FROM THE RICE PADDIES TO THE JUNGLE

Ed Dull

authorHOUSE®

AuthorHouse™
1663 Liberty Drive
Bloomington, IN 47403
www.authorhouse.com
Phone: 833-262-8899

This book is a work of non-fiction. Unless otherwise noted, the author and the publisher make no explicit guarantees as to the accuracy of the information contained in this book and in some cases, names of people and places have been altered to protect their privacy.

Published by AuthorHouse 12/06/2021

ISBN: 978-1-6655-4610-2 (sc)
ISBN: 978-1-6655-4612-6 (hc)
ISBN: 978-1-6655-4611-9 (e)

Library of Congress Control Number: 2021924415

Print information available on the last page.

Any people depicted in stock imagery provided by Getty Images are models, and such images are being used for illustrative purposes only. Certain stock imagery © Getty Images.

This book is printed on acid-free paper.

The five lieutenants of C-5-12/ 199th LIB
Hugh Foster, Bob Brenner, George Sheridan
Carey Walker, Ed Dull

Foreword

On August fourth, 1967, I graduated from Murray State University. After graduation, another ceremony was held at the school's ROTC department. Along with two other ROTC cadets, I was sworn in as an officer in the United States Army Reserves. I became a second lieutenant in the Army Infantry branch.

This commissioning also came with a two-year active-duty commitment. For the next two years I was an active-duty officer of the Army and would do what it wanted and needed of me. The first year consisted of attending the Infantry Officers Basic Course at Fort Benning, Georgia, followed by a tour at Fort Leonard Wood as a training officer. Then my orders came down from headquarters that my next assignment was to become part of the 199th Infantry Brigade in Bien Hoa, South Vietnam. Life changed for me for the next year.

When I returned from his tour of duty in South Vietnam, the protests of the anti-war movement made it impossible for the returning soldiers to acknowledge their time serving their country in a very unpopular war. That part of my life was left in a box filled with my letters home and personal memories. Like so many other returning soldiers, I did not talk much about that year. Unpopular war, unnerving thoughts.

After my parents had passed away, I found the packet of letters I had sent home. My parents had kept them and also collected the letters

I had sent to many of the people who were in correspondence with me during that year. I had also kept a journal of stories of that tour of duty.

Finally, after reading each of those letters I decided to merge the letters in chronological sequence with the stories. Many of the dates in the letters have been matched for accuracy with the After-Action Reports from the 199th Infantry's official website, Redcatcher.Org.

I hope this will give a personal insight of the life of an infantry platoon leader during the war in Vietnam. Each person's trip is different. This was mine.

CONTENTS

From the Rice Paddies to the Jungles

1. College time
   A. Dream
   B. ROTC
   C. Graduation
2. I am in the Army now
   A. IOBC and Ft. Leonard Wood
   B. Orders
   C. Benny Badgett
   D. Telling my parents
   E. Jungle School. Old friends reconnect and E and E.
3. What in the world is the 199th Infantry Brigade
   A. Formation at Ft. Benning
   B. Who was in charge.
   C. Formation of the 5th of the 12th.
   D. Location in Vietnam and the areas of operation.
   E. Concept of the Infantry light brigade.
4. Welcome to Vietnam
   A. Flight
   B. Intro to BMB and Camp Frenzell Jones
   C. Meet Battalion Commander
   D. Flight to C. 5/12
   E. First days with 1st platoon.
   F. Sgt. Joe Rush, Pruitt, Weenie, TA Riggins
   G. Combat: River patrol, 105 trip wire, wounded and swamp.
5. October-November
   A. Bridge construction repairs type of bridge, river around Saigon.

From The Rice Paddies To The Jungles

Chapter 1

College

The sun beat down mercilessly. It was hot. Over 100 degrees even though it was still morning. The sun was up and in full force with very few clouds to block its rays. No wind. Great day for a ground sweep!

I got word from my RTO (radio operator) that my platoon was to be point. The first ones in the area.

It was late morning and we were sweeping the area for any Viet Cong. We broke out of the jungle into a clearing the size of about two football fields. The good part of this was that we did not have to fight the thick vegetation of the jungle. The bad part was that now we were exposed to any enemy that might be watching. Now instead of just being noisy, we were also visible. The area was sawgrass about four feet high. Similar to the wheat fields back home except higher and the edges of the grass would cut like little blades. The only feature in this field was a lone thorn tree standing like a sentry in the middle of the open prairie.

Our orders were to cross and provide cover for the troops behind us.

We were to receive a supply drop from base camp and the helicopters would need a landing area. This was it. Open and available to land and drop the supplies. This meant food, clothing and water for the men. We would form a defensive perimeter around the landing zone to provide safety for the choppers to land.

My platoon went toward the tree. We were in single file and did not talk it was too hot to talk. The men were spaced out in proper formation. My RTO and I were in the middle after the first squad. I heard a commotion upfront. Everyone stopped and listened. Then the yelling and screaming started. A grenade exploded then the gunfire erupted. Both M-16 and AK-47 fire meant contact. I yelled for the men to spread out and cover the front squad. I was unable to raise the point man on the radio. I had the men advance slowly to get into contact with the first squad. The sawgrass kept us from seeing what was happening to our front. It was move by feel. Once we made contact with the first squad, I ordered the men to lay down fire. Aim to the front and keep a steady fire toward the enemy. The AK fire grew with steady force. It must be a large enemy unit we stumbled onto.

I was on the radio filling in the company commander with our status. The enemy rifle fire into our position was accurate. Low and accurate. These were trained soldiers, not the guerilla forces. The RTO was hit and so was the radio. It was disabled and no communication was available. The heat was worse since we were in the grass on our stomachs. No visibility and no air movement. The smell of gunpowder was noxious. The hot bullet casings ejected from the men's rifles would hit me and I did not notice their sting. I was yelling to my men to keep their position tight so the enemy could not advance through us. Suddenly, I felt a white-hot burning in my chest. I tried to move and was able to roll over and see the sky above through the haze of the gunpowder. The sky was not blue, rather white. It was hazy. The sound of the battle was fainter. Finally, I saw someone above me. Help at last! Was it the medic? There was a weapon, but it was an AK 47 with a bayonet. Not one of ours. It was aimed at me. Nothing else. Just blank and sweat!

The sweat was terrible. It was pouring off of me like a river. I woke up. I was not in Vietnam. It was the middle of winter and I was a senior in college at Murray State University in Murray, Kentucky. It was February, 1967. The temperature was cold. Kentucky in the winter was cold and snowy. This was no exception.

A dream. Thank God, not the real thing. Wait, I thought. When you die in a dream, you are really supposed to die. Well, I guess that was an old wives' tale. It had been so vivid though. The open field. The tree. The firefight. Now that I am awake, I might as well study for tomorrow's history test.

The next morning, I was talking with my best friend, Cully Gooden, a fellow ROTC student about the dream. He remarked that "aren't you supposed to die when that happens in a dream?" I replied "That is what I had always been told. Maybe we had seen that on Twilight Zone or something".

How did this even be a topic of conversation? Well, after an unpleasant two years at Westminster College, a small midwestern college, I wanted to change schools. Maybe it was a mutual idea between me and the Dean of Westminster College.

My sister and brother-in-law had both gone to Murray State University. It was a coed school (unlike Westminster College) and they agreed to accept me if I enrolled in the advanced ROTC program. Great, except I did not take the first two years of ROTC. Fortunately, the government had just started a new program. If a person would go through basic training in the Army at Fort Knox, Kentucky, then he could enter advanced Army ROTC at the college of his choice. I thought this was a good opportunity to start a new school and a new adventure.

Basic training was an eye opener. Men from all over the US were in our class. Forty of us were in this barracks that had been built as temporary barracks for WWII. Twenty bunks, each a double decker, with a wall locker and a foot locker per man to hold all of one's personal gear. A place for everything and everything in its place. Linoleum floors that were swept, waxed and cleaned each day by the troops. Clothing, boots, belts buckles and brass were issued to each of us. Then came polishing all of it to a brilliant shine. The brass was burned to remove the factory lacquer, then brought to a high shine with Brasso. Our boots were polished and waxed to an Army standard "spit polish". This process taught us to take pride in our military appearance as well as ourselves. Pride in our appearance was the goal.

Privacy was not existent. The bathroom consisted of ten toilet stools and ten urinals. All in a row with no dividers. It was interesting to have guys on the pot, smoking, reading the newspaper and talking nonchalantly about baseball scores. Modesty was gone. Instead of being an individual, we became a unit. As the sergeant said, time and time again, "You are not white, black or any other color except green!" Basic Training and military bearing must have had some effect, because at the end of the Basic training we each went to our separate colleges to be part of the advanced ROTC programs.

Advanced ROTC was a benefit to me and the other students. We signed a commitment to the Army for a two year active service obligation after graduation. The Army paid our tuition, books and room and board. We also received fifty dollars a month while we were in school. All we had to do was sign on the dotted line.

Military Science was also a minor counting toward hours to graduation. We had classes during the week, drills each Friday and weekend maneuvers twice a month to put into practical use the drill instructions we learned in class.

During the summer between our junior and senior years, each of the ROTC students attended advanced summer camps at Indiantown Gap Military Reservation in Pennsylvania. Murray State cadets were in the same camp as Virginia Military Institute, Virginia Tech and other top-notch military schools. The mix included some of the best ROTC students available outside of the Military Academies. I would cross paths with these people through my time in the military.

At the end of the camp and upon return to Murray State University each of us were required to commit to a branch of the Army. The Army consists of three combat arms; Infantry, the ground fighters; Armor, the tank drivers and Artillery, the cannon cockers. The other branches such as transportation, ordinance, chemical, medical service and supply are in place to make sure the combat arms can fight effectively. Most of the Army consists of the support branches for the combat arms. I believe that 90% are support and 10% actually fight. That being said, all troops fight when the need arises.

Murray State was known as a combat arms school. The emphasis was to provide the best infantry officers. I was encouraged to choose infantry as my branch. The speech went something like this: "If you go infantry then you are going to spend your two years of active duty in Germany. You will drink great beer, meet many young beautiful European ladies, buy a Volkswagen, drive all over Europe and bring the car home with good memories to last a lifetime. How can you go wrong?!" So, of course I signed my preference to be Infantry. You had three choices of branches, so I picked Infantry for all three. That car had my name written all over it!

Little did I know that the war in Vietnam was becoming a pressure cooker and we were inside. Lyndon Johnson had stated on July 28, 1965 that he was increasing the United States' presence in that country. At that time there were less than 50,000 troops in Country, but by 1967 there would be over 500,000 American soldiers in Vietnam.

I graduated from college in August 1967. After graduation ceremonies were complete, we proceeded to the Military Science Department. the Military Science (ROTC) graduates were commissioned as second lieutenants in a separate ceremony. There were three of us commissioned that day.

Chapter 2

I Am In The Army Now

My first duty assignment was Fort Benning Georgia. Officers Basic Course was an eight week course for newly minted Infantry second lieutenants. We went through tactics for small units (infantry platoon maneuvers). Many of the guys from Indiantown Gap were in this class. My roommate was Milt Culp. Milt was from Deland Florida. He would be wounded in Vietnam much later.

Next came my first duty assignment. Fort Leonard Wood, Missouri was in the middle of the state and known for being very cold in the winter and super hot in the summer. I reported into the Training Battalion and met my captain. He was a pipe smoking career Captain. I was assigned to lead an advanced infantry training platoon, including the persons who had been through the program more than once, or recycled personnel.

In addition to training officer, each officer had housekeeping jobs. One of my jobs was Mess Officer. This meant I oversaw food preparation for the company. It was brought to my attention that we had too much bread. When in doubt ask the professional! I asked the head cook how we could remedy this problem. He said" let's make bread pudding!". By the end of the week everyone had their fill of bread pudding.

One of my high school friends was taking advanced training at

Leonard Wood. I had received word that Benny Badgett was on base. Over the Fourth of July I was planning to go to Lake of the Ozarks for a weekend. Benny was at his barracks and did not have authorization to leave for the weekend. I was in summer uniform and went to his front office. As an officer nobody questioned my being there. I talked to the noncommissioned officer in charge and stated that private Badgett was needed for a project for the next day or two. No problem. He was summoned with overnight gear and off we went to the lake. It was not a lot but the best I could do. It also gave Benny some time away from the military.

The first year was rounded out at Leonard Wood. In August I was given orders for Vietnam. My assignment was for Headquarters B Company, 5th Battalion 12th Infantry, 199th Infantry Brigade. Long Bien, Vietnam.

When I told my family of the new assignment, they were quite concerned. A number of guys from my home town of Mt. Vernon, Illinois had served in the conflict and some did not return.

I spent leave time in Mt. Vernon. The last night before I shipped out, a number of friends from high school were together at Rosie's Pizza Roma Lounge. Both Raymond Baril and Larry "Bo" White were there. They had returned from their tour in Vietnam. Bo looked at me and said "Well guy, you are going to be a platoon leader for a line infantry platoon? It has been nice knowing you! "He was not trying to be snide or mean, just words coming out of one who knew the score. That did not help the mood. I went home and was with family until I left.

The first leg of the trip was a two week stay at Fort Davis, Panama Canal Zone for Jungle Warfare School. Most infantry officers and infantry NCOs for their first tour went through the course. The climate was similar to Vietnam. It is on the equator. The jungle was thick and the terrain was similar to swampy lands.

The weekend before classes started, the soldiers went to Colon, the major city on the Panama Canal. We walked around sampling the sights and the foods from the street vendors. On Monday, one of the first classes was on how to survive with jungle food. Nature provides a bounty; it is there for our taking. The Sergeant asked the class "who has eaten Iguana meat?" Nobody raised their hands. He next asked "Who went to Colon this weekend?" All raised our hands. "Who had the chicken on a stick from the street vendors hibachis?" All raised their hands. "Now that we know you have eaten Iguana meat; it was not too bad, was it?" Intro to jungle foods. The next two weeks were exercises in how to lay ambushes, river crossings and surviving in a jungle environment. The last part of the program was a two day escape and evasion course that led for a number of kilometers through jungle. We started in four man teams. At the start, we were attacked by mock hostile forces. One of the sergeants from my team took off through the jungle and ran off the edge of a cliff breaking a couple of ribs. We stayed with him until he could be evacuated. In doing so we were captured and interrogated. Then we were released to complete the course. The course was a morale and confidence booster.

CHAPTER 3

WHAT IN THE WORLD IS THE 199TH INFANTRY BRIGADE??

My orders came through that I was to be sent to the 199th Infantry Brigade, Company B, 5th battalion 12th Infantry, 199th Infantry Brigade. APO San Francisco, Ca. 96279. This unfortunately, did not mean I was being transferred to San Francisco, California. All troops being sent to Vietnam were routed through San Francisco. Oh well!

What in the world was the 199th Infantry Brigade anyway? I had grown up hearing about the Big Red One (First Infantry Division), the Screaming Eagles (the 101st Airborne Division) and the 82nd Airborne, the All Americans. In my short military career, I had not encountered the 199th Infantry Brigade. Maybe that is a good thing? Maybe they are a rear unit to help out in the staging areas to support the troops that did the real fighting.

So, I began checking up on who this new group was to which I was being attached. That was an eye opener.

The 199th Infantry Brigade, (Separate), (Light) had a short but very illustrious history. It was formed on June First, 1966 in Fort Benning Georgia. The concept of the Light infantry Brigade was to have a small flexible fighting unit that can be pulled from one location and transported to an entirely different location and be up, ready, fully functional and fighting in a matter of 24 hours. It was called a hitchhiker unit to be able to be attached to other units or filling the gaps where a fighting unit could quickly function. That meant it did not carry much heavy equipment. The artillery was confined to 105 Howitzers that could be dropped or moved in place quickly to support the ground troops, infantry and mobile (armored personnel carriers) at a moment's notice.

In 1966 it came to Vietnam as two battalions, the 2nd of the 3rd infantry (part of the Old Guard that guards the Tomb of the Unknown Soldier) and the 3rd of the 7th infantry. In the next few months, the 4th battalion 12th Infantry was formed and added. Finally, in 1967 the 5th battalion 12th Infantry was formed. It was shipped to Vietnam in April 1968.There were also numerous support units that were part of the Brigade. These supported, transported and kept the foot soldiers functioning.

The unit became based at Camp Frenzell-Jones located in Long Bien, about 20 miles west of Saigon. The camp was named for one of the first casualties within the Brigade. This camp was also known as Brigade Main Base (BMB). The Brigade structure was located in what became a sprawling tent city. From the BMB troops were sent to guard locations through an area ranging on the east to Vung Tau, to the west Parrots Beak (Cambodian Border). From the north just south of Cu Chi (known later for the tunnel systems) to the south, the Mekong Delta (home of the 9th Infantry Division, the Riverines because of the marshy swampy terrain and the use of boats to traverse the swamps). In 1970 The 199th was one of the spearhead units that entered into Cambodia and set up base camps to directly encounter the North Vietnamese using that route as part of the Ho Chi Minh Trail.

The troops from the different battalions would be located at different encampments throughout the area of operation. There were Firebases which guarded villages and routes into and out of Saigon. Small platoon sized encampments that guarded bridges and water routes through the area. These are the locations where most of the infantry soldiers slept and remained during their tours of duty in Vietnam.

Although the 199th had a short history after formation, the footprint was huge in the Vietnam War. During it's time in country four of the soldiers were awarded the Medal of Honor for gallantry in combat. Eleven more soldiers were awarded the Distinguished Service Cross for gallantry in combat. Not just the line soldiers were in combat, but the senior officers were exposed as well. One of the Battalion Commanders was killed in action. During the time this unit was in country, until it was disbanded in 1970, a total of 757 of its soldiers were killed in combat. This was a storied fighting unit.

CHAPTER 4

WELCOME TO VIETNAM

Next was the flight to the Republic of Vietnam. My flight was a TWA 707. First to Honolulu, then Guam and finally to Tan San Nhut Airbase. Our plane was filled with soldiers. No civilians were in sight. The flight crew was experienced. The stewardesses were older than I had seen on other flights. They were very professional with a plane full of soldiers.

The nerves on board were pretty severe once we left Guam. Next stop was the war. Our flight was delayed landing as the pilot announced a slight delay since the Tan San Nhut airbase was under a rocket attack. I fully expected once we landed that someone would issue us a rifle, helmet and flak jacket when we hit the ground. When the doors opened though, the soldiers were in khaki uniforms with regular headgear and no weapons to be seen. Just like stateside except we were in a war zone.

We were ushered to busses and sent to the Replacement Center north of Saigon; a huge dusty hot city teaming with a country full of displaced people in the center of South Vietnam. We were told to keep the windows of the bus open and our arms inside the bus. Supposedly, the locals would cut off any ring fingers to get the rings and take the watches any way possible. Great introduction to our new home.

At the Replacement Center, I was placed on a Deuce and a half (2-and-a-half-ton truck) and sent to the Brigade Main Base (Camp

Frenzell-Jones) at Long Binh. This was about 15 miles northwest of Saigon.

My orders were to be attached to Company B, 5th Battalion 12th Infantry. Instead, I was assigned to Company C of the same unit as a platoon leader.

While waiting for the flight to go into the field to meet my new unit the new replacements were to go through an acclimation period. This was a short course in adjusting to Vietnam.

One part of the acclimation was going through an obstacle course to acquaint the soldiers with various booby traps the Viet Cong used against our troops. There were different types, ranging from punji sticks made of bamboo hidden in the brush, to pits filled with these bamboo spikes. There were also grenades that had the pins pulled and stuck in empty C ration cans with a string tied around the top of the grenade. These were set across a path so when tripped, the grenade came out of the can and detonated close to the tripper. Unfortunately, the course was closed shortly after I arrived in country. It seems the Viet Cong had gone into the course and rigged some extra booby traps that exploded, wounding our soldiers while they were going through the course. This made us realize that the war zone was everywhere we were in this country. There were no set boundaries where the good guys were and the enemy was located. We were indeed strangers in a strange land. The Vietnamese around our base camp were not all on our side.

During TET 1968, (The Lunar New Year, usually at the end of January or during February) the Viet Cong attacked the Brigade Main Base in force. Since the line troops, who were the main fighting force, were deployed in the field, this left the support staff to defend the base. The cooks, typists and other support personnel held fast and repelled great numbers of Viet Cong. After the major battles were finished, one of the Viet Cong commanders was found dead at the wire around the base. It was a barber from the base who had been able to listen to the different commanders discuss tactics while getting their hair cut. The enemy was everywhere.

Brigade Main Base was a city within itself. The barracks were wood sides and wood floors. The windows could be raised as flaps and the doors were screened.

Each officers' building held four bunks with cots and mattresses. There were community showers and outhouses for sitting while doing your business. If the need was just to relieve yourself there was a circle of cardboard 105 mm howitzer shell casings tubes with the bottoms cut out and punched in the ground to catch the urine. It was limed daily to decrease the smell. Again, no privacy.

The Battalion and Brigade offices were permanent wood structures. Each Battalion had its own area. I was housed in the 5th of the 12th area. Here I drew supplies to prepare to go into the field. After a few days getting acclimated, I was directed to the Battalion Commander's office.

I met with Lt. Colonel Herbert Ray. He was about 40 or so years old. Tall, gaunt, white haired and stern. He had been wounded 2 months before I came in country during a river boat operation in the Mekong Delta area. The boat he was commanding from was attacked and he was wounded during the firefight. Lt. Colonel Ray was fiercely protective of his battalion. We went through the introductions and then he said it was time to go to meet the company commander and my new platoon.

We flew to the area called the Pineapple which was west of Saigon. His light observation helicopter (loch) was flying close to the deck to avoid being a good target for snipers. I noticed large holes in the otherwise symmetrical rice paddies on the way to my new firebase home. Peaceful, yet definitely a war zone. What a contrast. People were in the fields tending the rice crops which at that time were under water and contained by dikes, making nice squares, interrupted by the bomb craters. We would fly over the villages consisting of 10 or 15 thatched one room huts surrounded by the rice paddies like little islands surrounded by a sea of rice. There were canals that acted as roadways of water between the villages and the rice paddies. This made travelling by boats a necessity.

We flew into the firebase that was to be my home. On the way there, Lt Colonel Ray asked me the most penetrating question. "These are good men. They have been in battle. Are you good enough to lead them?" My answer was "yes", but I questioned it and I believe that was what I strived for the whole next year!!

We landed at the edge of the base. Then we proceeded to the command hooch. There we met with Captain McPherson Elliott. He had been in country on a previous tour, before most troops. He had described Saigon as a beautiful city of about two hundred thousand persons with a Parisian influence. Of course, now it was a war-torn city of over one million displaced persons.

Captain Elliott greeted me and directed me to the first platoon. They had recently lost their platoon leader, who was killed in an explosive's accident.

The Lt. Colonel left and Captain Elliott walked with me to the first platoon location. We went to the command hooch, my new home and met with the staff. Sergeant Joe Rush was my new platoon Sergeant. Joe had been in the army for years and was on his first of two tours in country. Joe was known throughout the battalion as a top soldier. The assistant platoon Sergeant was staff Sergeant Pruitt. Pruitt had been with the First Infantry Division on his previous tour in country. Both were very seasoned and competent soldiers.

They introduced me to my platoon. Sergeant Weenie McClain was first squad leader. Weenie had been in country for over seven months.

I asked how he got the nickname Weenie. He looked and grinned and said "Size does matter!" The next soldier was TA 50 Riggins, a corporal. He was so named after the web belt we wore. All of the items are hooked to the belt so when we go to the field, just put on the belt and your gear is in place. It seemed that when he was first in country, he hooked all the gear to his web belt and when it was put on it was upside down and had to be restrung properly. He also kept on that belt every kind of equipment the Army had issued. (TA-50 is the acronym for Table of Authorization #50, which is the authorization document for miscellaneous equipment issued to soldiers, such as ammo pouches, first aid packet). So, we are hung with different monikers. Again, both Weenie and TA were battle hardened and very good soldiers.

After I had been introduced and put my gear in the command hooch, Joe asked if I wanted to go on a recon of the base and a short patrol outside of the perimeter? Not really, but now was as good a time as any. I went with Weenie and his squad on a short patrol of the area. It was a good introduction to life as a platoon leader. Most of the time it is best to follow the lead of the people who are knowledgeable and are still around. Then learn before showing my ignorance. I had heard and firmly believe that if you keep your mouth shut and eyes open it is harder for people to know how stupid you are. If you open your mouth, it only confirms their suspicions!!

The firebase was company sized. It held the sleeping quarters for four infantry platoons as well as a battery of 105 howitzers. Each platoon was supposed to have 40 men, two sergeants and one platoon leader. Due to many factors, this was never the case. Usually, we had about 25 to 30 men in each line platoon.

The infantry company had three line platoons and one platoon of 81mm mortars that were taken into the field on major movements. The exterior of the firebase was dirt revetments topped with sandbags and ammo boxes filled with dirt. Each platoon had one command hooch made with ammo boxes filled with dirt and then topped with sandbags and a metal top of road planking covered with layers of sandbags. The squads had two man hooches made with ammo box bases then covered with metal culvert tiles and covered with sandbags. The floors were either dirt or a pallet to keep your feet off the mud floor. Each end of the hooch was covered with sandbags that acted as blast deflectors from mortar fire. Most men had either a bed of ammo boxes or used their hammocks strung inside the hooch. There was room for very little personal gear. Normally the troops had one spare uniform, socks and a spot for hygiene gear.

I got into stride over the next few weeks with briefings from our company commander, getting to know my men and the other platoon leaders. We would have daily patrols, evening ambush locations and keeping perimeter guards for protection of the firebase.

At the end of September, the battalion was tasked with a two day river patrol and cordon of a village. This was my first encounter with the Mike boats. These were troop carriers similar to the ones seen in the Normandy invasion. Each boat was open and had a ramp that dropped to the shore for entry and exit. They carried two platoons per boat There were M-60 machine guns on the bottom level and two 50 caliber machine guns on the second level near the driver's cabin.

On this patrol my platoon also had company commander Elliott and the company command post. The first night we deployed in a swampy area. We deployed, made a perimeter around the boats and waited until dawn to proceed with the mission. The high ground was still about 6 inches under water. Many of the men sat on their helmets just to keep their rear ends dry. At dawn we reimbarked the boats and went up river to an area of thick brush. Our purpose was to disembark and go through the thick brush behind the village to keep VC from fleeing out the back while the main force searched the village. The boat beached and the ramp started to go down. Captain Elliott yelled "Stop the ramp!!". We all froze. Our platoon was at the front of the boat ready to take off. Nobody moved. What was happening? Then we looked and saw the ramp was pulling on a wire as it was being lowered. Elliott had seen some movement of the wire. It was traced to an unexploded 105 howitzer shell set up as a booby trap. If the wire had been tripped the explosion would have been directed at our exposed troops. The ramp was raised and slowly the boat backed off the shore. We were then directed to moor with the main boarding party and make the cordon inland.

The troops were in pace and the search began. Soon after an explosion rocked the area. We were on high alert. One of the search platoons, not in our company, had taken a break and sat by a tree for a rest. The RTO (radio operator) had triggered a grenade booby trap. His radio had taken the brunt of the explosion but he was still severely wounded. Five others were also wounded. They were brought on to a Mike boat and treated by the medics. Dust-off choppers were called to take them to Saigon to the hospital. I believe one of the soldiers did not make it. The others survived. The cordon was completed and no contact with the Viet Cong was made. We stayed in place that night and the next morning hot food was flown in for the troops. After eating, we returned to the Mike boats and went to our firebase. So that was my introduction to war at its unexpected time and an understanding that we were enemies in a hostile land at all times.

The weather in our area was called the wind down of the monsoons. Rain would come in the morning for a short time and also in the afternoon. Sunshine in between. Hot, muggy and soggy all the time. When I arrived in country, I weighed 160 pounds. My waist was a pleasant 36 inches. After some time in the heat and with the patrols and eating c-rations two meals out of three, I went down to 140 pounds and a 28-inch waist. Even though I had lost the weight I still kept my tummy. Hence the affectionate(?) name of Lt. Fatty!

A couple of weeks after the cordon operation my platoon was on our daily patrol. The patrol was a cloverleaf with one squad going to the left, making a circle, the next going to the front doing the same and the third going to the right returning to the center. One squad would stay at the firebase to keep security and keep them fresh in case we needed reserves. Contact was made by the second squad, the forward element. They saw 6 people in conical hats and black pajamas. Were they farmers? No, they had AK-47s not hoes and rakes. I gave permission to make contact. A firefight began. It started slowly, a few shots. Then return fire, then sounds like a string of firecrackers then a din of sounds. It lasted less than 30 minutes total. The rest of the platoon began to make a sweep of the area to drive any remaining enemy into the firing zone. It was amazing that the fight was being controlled on so many levels. My company commander was on my radio. Then there was a break into the radio from the battalion commander., who was in his helicopter. Finally, we heard on our radio "This is Redcatcher 1" the Brigade commander, General Davison. Each giving directions and wanting a report. Thank goodness the fight did not last long. It seemed like using a bomb to kill a mosquito. But it was much better than not having support when we would need it. Our command was protective of our troops and wanted us safe and superior in power when possible.

We swept and found one VC killed. None of my men were killed or wounded. The cool heads on the ground, Sgt Rush and Sgt. Pruitt made sure all the men were accounted for and that we thoroughly swept the area to prevent any stragglers from escaping or sniping to cause casualties. Pruitt got on the radio to begin the housekeeping duties. He ordered M-16 and .30 caliber bullets and grenades. Finally, he ordered clean uniforms for each of us, including myself. I asked him "Why are you ordering uniforms for all of us. We have not had any casualties?"

Pruitt looked at me, spit out a chaw of his tobacco and said" Well, sir, you mean you did not piss your pants during the firefight?"

I was a little insulted and said "Of course not, I was too busy to be that scared!"

Another chaw and that certain look, you know the one where someone just did not understand the basics: "Sir, it is not being scared. When you get into a situation like this, just relieve yourself! If you get gut shot then it does not explode your bladder and cause you peritonitis!"

"Oh!" Enough said. Put that on the list for the future. Every day is a learning experience. That is just one more reason why officers listen to their sergeants. They talk from experience. These are just some of the things not taught in ROTC or Officers' Basic Course. Stay alive to fight another day!

Ed Dull

September 25, 1968

Dear Mom and Dad,

Well, at last I'm home. I'm in the 5th Battalion, 12th Infantry, 199th Infantry Brigade. I've not been assigned my company or platoon yet. They are giving us time to get our clothes fixed and settled in our BOQ!! (Which consists of tents built for 4 and accommodate 5 of us and our foot lockers, but don't have a wall locker yet.

We landed at Bien Hoa Sunday, time change, we are one day ahead of you. Then we went to the 90th Replacement Company at Long Binh for our assignments. Early Monday morning the 199th picked us up and brough us to the brigade Main Base camp. It is still in Long Binh. That is for our unit assignments. This place is fantastic, we have a great Officers Club. Last night they had a live band that was great! There is a large swimming pool and miniature golf course about two blocks from where I live. And a large snack bar.

Right now, I am going to school AGAIN!!It is a one week refresher course for all new personnel. The mission of our unit (Brigade) at the present is to defend Saigon's South and East sides. It is pretty easy duty. I will be moving down there next Monday and joining my new unit. I probably won't be back here for about a month. Most of my gear I will take with me. Just civilian clothing and a few extras I will leave here.

Gotta go to class now. Take care and be good.

Love,

Ed

CHAPTER 5

OCTOBER-NOVEMBER

During October our company was moved from the firebase to Bridge duty in Saigon. My platoon was positioned on Bridge Number 4 which was a large iron structure across one of the main rivers bisecting Saigon. The river was the Mekong. It was a major shipping route into and out of Saigon. The bridge entrances on either side consisted of residences and businesses. Traffic was heavy and constant all day long. Vehicles ranging from bicycles to semi-tractor trailers were always in motion as well as pedestrian traffic on the sides of the bridge.

The men in our unit were positioned at each end of the bridge and contact was maintained through my command post in the center of the bridge with the PRC 25 radios from each squad. During the day and night, we had men patrol the length of the bridge to inspect for sappers or persons attempting to sabotage the bridge and disrupt commerce. As the men would patrol the bridge, they would at various time drop one pound blocks of TNT with 30 second timers off the bridge into the river. If there were any scuba divers or small craft underneath, it would shock or sink them. The 30 second fuses allowed the dynamite to actually hit the water before detonation.

We just had to make sure there were no transport ships under the area we bombed.

The bridge was opened at six am each day. At dusk (about 5 or so depending on the season, we would shut it down and nobody crossed without permission. One evening shortly after we closed the bridge, I received a call from one of my sentries. "Sir, there is a jeep with an officer and driver that are requesting permission to cross into Saigon." "I will be there immediately."

I hiked to the end of the bridge and sure enough a very impatient driver wanted to get his first lieutenant across. I asked what the purpose was and he responded that the Lieutenant was going to rotate back to the States and his plane was leaving late today. I went around to check them out and the lieutenant was my former roommate from college, Elvin "Sonny" Blaisdell. He had gotten a late start from his base and was supposed to be on a late flight out of Tan San Knut air base at Long Bien. Special circumstances require special action. I let them cross on the condition they took me to the middle of the bridge. Done! I wished him well and it was nice to see a familiar face make it back home.

With the extensive traffic from daily use, the bridge needed constant maintenance. The bridge roadway was a steel and asphalt surface. Like any other road potholes were common. I was amazed to see how the road crews filled them. Instead of having the hot asphalt trailers with the rock and steamy oily mixture, the crew would take a chunk of tar and rock mix that had been taken from another street and fill the hole. Then they would take a blow torch affair and heat the pile until it was malleable and mend the hole. I thought it was a primitive method, but the mix worked for the time we were on the bridge.

At night not only the bridge was closed to traffic, but also the area around the ends of the bridge were under curfew. It was like a ghost town. The night animals were out along the wharf areas below the bridge. Large rats crept around. Occasionally, the men would take a shot at the rats. The bridge was safe during the time we guarded it.

In November we moved again. This time it was to the area at the Western edge of Vietnam called the Parrots Beak. It is named since it does look like a parrot's head and beak. This area separated Vietnam and Cambodia. Our firebase was at the south edge of a Michelin rubber plantation. The plantation had been there since the French had been in Vietnam. The rubber trees were huge and the plantation was very dense. It had roads and trail throughout the plantation. It was also off limits for the Americans to conduct any actions within the borders. We were warned that under no circumstance were we to patrol, set up ambushes and even to fire our weapons into the plantation. It might harm the trees.

Unfortunately, the Viet Cong did not receive this memo. Occasionally, we would receive sniper fire from the plantation The conversation would go something like "Charlie base, we have incoming fire". "Charlie One, where is this fire coming from?" It is coming from the north of the firebase." "Charlie one, is that the rubber plantation?" "That's affirmative"

"You are not to engage them, do you understand?" "Yes, of course."" Will you talk to someone and have them cease fire?" "No".

Such was the cooperation. One day I was a little upset when it started. I told the guard to engage. He did and the firing stopped. About 15 minutes later I got a call on the radio from Charlie base: "Charlie One, did you fire into the rubber plantation? We are getting reports from the managers that they are getting fire from the firebase area!!" "No, "I replied. "Not from us. We were getting fire from the south of the firebase that went over our position and must have landed in the plantation." There was silence for a while. No more sniper fire from that location for a while and nothing more was said from our base either. I think I got lucky on that one.

We would patrol the area throughout the Parrot's beak. The area was flat and had a mix of rice paddies and brushy areas. The rains had stopped and the ground was becoming firm. It was a lot easier to move. In the area called the Plain of Reeds the brush was taller that the height of the men. It was brutal patrolling through them. On one occasion we stopped and I had the men fan out for a short rest. One of the men, Sergeant Green, let out a scream. Rifles at the ready, I went over to hm. "What is the problem Sgt Green?" "Sir", he responded, "I sat down on a log and it moved!" We looked and the "log was the longest snake I had ever seen. It must have been an anaconda, many feet long. The break was over, time to move out and look out for the snake.

On another sweep of the same area, we believed there were some Viet Cong in the brush, but it was so thick we could not tell if or where they were. I set up men on one side of the heavy brush and at the far end where it had thinned out. Normally I carried two white phosphorous grenades. Nobody wanted to take them since they not only exploded when armed but also the phosphorous burned hot and could not be easily extinguished. The wind was blowing toward the men in the thinned-out area so they were safe from any flames. The fires started just fine. Since it was dry the brush caught instantly.

Unfortunately, the wind then shifted and the fire was coming toward my squads. "Retreat!!!" I yelled at the men. We went full tilt the other way. Fortunately, there was a creek with water we dove into. The fire died out and we were singed but not otherwise injured. The result, after we regrouped was that there were no Viet Cong there and we did clear the area and took away their concealment. We also wore smoky uniforms until we could return to base.

On another occasion we were to cross over the edge of the Beak to the west. This was technically into Cambodia. We spent a couple of days patrolling the area. At that time, we had embedded two reporters, one from Playboy Magazine and one other publication. At no time during our briefings were we to discuss which side of the border we were located with either our men or the reporters. The sweeps went smoothly and no contact with any hostile forces was made. The reporters went on their way and they were out of our mind.

About a month later, one of my men received a letter from home. His mother attached a newspaper article and a picture of our platoon. She had circled his picture and asked "Is this you?" I took it to our company commander. He about flipped! The article was headed: "Are American Troops in Cambodia?" We assured that soldier that was not Cambodia and he was to tell his mother it was NOT him. Nothing more was said about that article from anyone!

One day a strange helicopter landed at the firebase carrying a Major who asked for me. That is normally not a good sign. Either I am in trouble from someone in authority or there is bad news from home. When we met, he asked if I had written my family recently? I had been a little dilatory in my writing skill recently. He explained that the head of the Red Cross in my home town had grown concerned and sent a formal request making sure I was not injured and unable to write.

I lived in a small town and my parents were social friends with the lady who was in charge of the Red Cross. I am sure that when my mother had expressed concern to her friend, the friend said she would get to the bottom of it.

Well, the next thing I knew, I was on a helicopter to Saigon. I was deposited at the building with rows of pay telephones. You would pay the good person at the desk twenty dollars (most of my retained money) and then you got a 5-minute call. I called my dad's office and he was not there, but I spoke with his secretary and told her I was ok. Please call my mother and let her know. The call was over. I was unceremoniously returned to my firebase and started writing home more diligently!!

As a first lieutenant, my pay was $450 per month. When combat zone pay (also known as hazardous duty pay) was added it totaled $550. Most of my tour was in the field, so there was little to spend money on. I kept $50 per month and sent the rest home to be deposited for the future. Usually, the $50 was plenty to keep me going for the month. The only time money was needed was when I went to brigade Main base for the officers' club, Saigon for a day out of the field, to go to the Cholon PX for supplies, or finally, for R&R, either in country or the one we got out of country.

Since we were in a foreign country and also a military presence in that country, American money, greenbacks, were not allowed. The rationale was supposedly that using our money would weaken the other country's monetary system.

The Vietnamese money consisted of piastres and dong. One hundred piastres equaled one dong. A dong was close to one American dollar. Since the country was in the midst of a civil war the economy was not very stable and that value fluctuated each day. Instead of being paid in the Vietnamese currency, all US soldiers were paid in money issued by the American government called Military Payment Currency, called MPC for short. This money was only to be paid and used on base and at the Military locations such as the USO in Saigon and the PX in Cholon. The military was not to use the MPC in open trade with the Vietnamese. The MPC was backed by the US Government and was the most stable currency other than the forbidden greenbacks. Therefore, the MPC and the Greenback were specifically sought out by the Vietnamese and were at a premium when buying goods and trade items on the open market. If an item cost ten dong, then by using MPC it could be purchased for about seven or eight MPC dollars. Greenbacks even had more value.

The American soldiers also had ration cards for goods deemed as necessary for them. Each soldier was allowed four cartons of cigarettes at the discounted prices of a dollar a carton. We were also allowed to purchase two bottles of liquor each month. The liquor was able to be purchased but could not be brought out to the field since it affected the soldiers' ability to be focused and fight. As a field soldier, we would receive four cigarettes in each c-ration meal pack, so the ration of cigarettes was not always necessary. This meant the rationed cigarettes were great for bargaining with the local Vietnamese population. It was good for getting haircuts as well as uniform cleaning, snacks, sodas and buying souvenirs and jewelry. The Vietnamese had a voracious appetite for cigarettes! The main trade item was for Salem Cigarettes. Menthol was new and Salem was the cigarette of choice for the population.

Since the MPC was not allowed to be used by the local population, it quickly became the most sought-after payment method among the local population. This held true more in the city of Saigon than in the villages. The currencies mixed quickly and frequently. During 1969 our government needed to make the MPC more secure. The only way to do that was to make an MPC change in one day countrywide. This was a huge and very secret undertaking no soldier was supposed to be allowed over five thousand dollars in MPC on their person.

The bases throughout Vietnam were secured one day and all money the soldiers had in their possession could be exchanged for the new MPC up to the maximum amount allowed at that time. Nonmilitary persons were not allowed to exchange MPC on any military base. For most soldiers this was not a problem. The soldiers in the field did not have much money on their person. I had one hundred dollars in my footlocker at the Brigade Main Base. I authorized one of our rear area personnel to break the lock on the footlocker and retrieve the money and hold it for me until I returned to collect it.

Since we were on patrol in the field and had no access to our base on the day of the exchange, we were granted one additional day to make the change upon returning to our firebase. When we returned to the firebase, the local villagers who had MPC in their possession tried to have us take their money, exchange it for them and return them new MPC or piastres. Some soldiers profited by doing this, although it was illegal and could cause them much trouble.

The soldiers in Saigon often traded much more freely with the local citizens. The mix of MPC as well as greenbacks was much more prevalent in the city than the field soldiers. Some military personnel were involved in the black market and also with prostitutes. Some of the soldiers had much more than the allowed currency. Any excess was worthless the day after the exchange. There were stories about rear echelon soldiers (the ones in Saigon and other cities) who lost thousands of dollars on the exchange day. Served them right!! After that day, I tried to make sure my men kept their MPC separate from the local currency. The best trade items were still good old Salems and other cigarettes.

October 9, 1968

Dear Mom and Dad,

I finally have a platoon and they are very good men too. Most of them are quite young. Some just 18 and 19, but they are the best soldiers around!

We went on a 3 day mission in a place just west of Saigon called the Pineapple. On Sunday, Monday and Tuesday. This morning we came back here to our perimeter. I didn't lose anyone but second platoon lost seven men on booby traps; none hurt seriously. We missed getting hit by an RPG (a rocket) mine by about four feet. Really tense, but no sweat.

My company commander is a very competent and conscientious man. It is his third tour in Vietnam and he is doing a great job. His name is Captain Elliott.

We have been listening to the World Series on the radio. It comes on at 1:15 in the morning. The Cards really seem to be giving them the works so far; it's only the 9th of October over here so I won't know the results until tonight.

There is a kid in the company that used to live in Mt. Vernon. He has relatives still there. His name is Merriman and has some relatives that live in Ina and Bluford. Isn't it a small world?

Give regards to everyone back home. It is a very different country. I will be sending you pictures of it later on. Maybe you could give some to Suzie Blades for her history project in school. It is on, of all things, our war in Vietnam. OK?

Gotta go now, we are cooking steaks for dinner tonight and I have to supervise to make sure mine is cooked the way Joe does it. Seared for about two on each side and simmered to a light medium rare.

Went swimming yesterday in the river right next to our position. It is not exactly clean water, but was cleaner than me when we came off the operation. Made me feel good. Well, that is about all for now. Don't worry about Old Ed, this is strictly a party, it's not as bad as everyone says. Take care. P.S. Send all mail airmail. Otherwise, it takes 31 days to get here. OK?

Love,

Ed

Ed Dull

October, 1968

Dear Dad and Mom,

Hi folks. I got the package yesterday and I want to tell you that it was really good! I like the chocolate chip cookies especially, same as usual!

The funniest thing happened last week while we were still on bridge duty. I was officer in charge of the bridge and a first lieutenant drove by about dark. I could never forget the outline of that face! It was Sonny Blaisdell, my roommate from Murray State. He stopped and talked for a while. He is working with the 9th division south of Saigon. It was really good to see him again.

Now we are in a different location south of Saigon. We're at Nha Be in a company position in the boondocks. It's not too bad except very hot.

Tonight, a funny thing happened. The ARVN (South Vietnamese), outpost about a hundred meters from my location started firing a machine gun across our platoon position about 6 feet over our heads. It really hacked us off and, being the platoon leader, I had to straighten them out. I went over there and politely told them that if the EVER fired at my men or position again that I would have their position mortared and everyone who came out of their area we would kill on the run. You know we have not had any trouble with them since then and I doubt if we will in the future. I still don't think Norman Vincent Peale would approve of my methods of friendly persuasion though?

That's about all this kid has to say except please tell me the address of Mr. and Mrs. Jack Crouch. I would like to send them a note. It is the least I could do for their thoughtfulness of me. They sent me a goodie box. Even though they lost their son they are still thinking about people like me.

Also, I've written to Frankie and got things straightened out. I still like her a lot but cannot decide which girl I want. Ain't that a tough decision to make while I am fighting a war? Got a letter from Aunt Dorothy today. I already wrote her. Gotta go now and get some sleep. Take care and God Bless you both!

Love,
Ed

32

October 1968

Dear Dad and Mom,

Hi folks, nothing much is happening here. We went back to the Pineapple plantation yesterday. We blew a few bunkers. We should have gotten some VC but they Di-Di'ed (got the hell out) before we landed. We were picked up to come back here to the bridge at 1400 in the afternoon (2 pm for you civilians!!)

I got the birthday present yesterday and the newspaper clipping. I liked the first better than the second. The socks I won't be able to wear for about 5 months because they are too light to wear under boots, but the checkered table cloth is something else! Everybody goes nuts when I bring it out. All gold and white. That definitely is OK! About the cigars Dad, as the saying goes "A woman is always just a woman, but a good cigar is a GREAT Smoke!!" These are definitely good cigars! I have already smoked two!

Other than that Frankie sent me a birthday present that was really sweet. She is an ok girl and I think the world of her but it is an awfully big world and I still have a lot of it to see.

I'd best go now. I'm at work again and better start working. Take care of yourselves. I'm doing the same.

Love,

Ed

Ed Dull

October, 1968

Dear Mom and Dad,'

    Hi. How are you? I am fine.

    Just a short note to tell you that: WAR IS HELL!!!

                                         Your Loving Son,
                                              Ed

October, 1968

Dear Dad and Mom,

Just a small letter to tell you that I am doing fine. Got your letter yesterday and one from Bobbie. I appreciated it very much. Sorry about the Cardinals losing the series. They just couldn't quite cut it this year, I guess. Maybe next year we will all go to see the games.

Life is easy around here. Last Wednesday we went on a recon patrol and found signs of VC but no action. Sunday, we went on a night ambush and made no contact. It's a good thing though. We were not well positioned. After the ambush we had to go about 100 meters through the rice paddies. That wasn't bad but mud was ankle deep in some areas, knee deep in some areas and waist deep and water was shoulder deep and sometimes over our head. It took quite a while to get there, needless to say, but nobody lost too much equipment.

Sunday, we came into Saigon and took over the main bridge leading into Saigon from Nha be. We use two full platoons to guard it. It really is easy living. I work 24 hours and am off for 24 hours. We are living in Camp Davis outside Saigon. This place is fantastic. It even has commodes that flush and that is rare here! We should be here for about a month or so until the rainy season ends completely.

I made first lieutenant yesterday. I should get my combat infantryman's badge (CIB) in a couple of weeks. I was sweating the first lieutenant rank since I made the Colonel pretty irritated the other day. But, I got it anyway. No sweat!

A guy I went to school with at Murray State is down here giving classes to my men this week. Just like home.

Gotta go now. I am officer in charge of this bridge now.

Love,
Ed

Ed Dull

Dear Patsy, Roger and Kids:

I want to thank you all for the birthday card. It really helps a lot to know someone is thinking enough about you to write!

Really, mail around here is just about the most important thing to the men (except DEROS which means "date expected to Return from Overseas")!

As far as that picture goes that you saw and were commenting on, it must have been a touched-up photo. The real thing just is not that good. I doubt David will be seeing me on TV. We haven't made that much contact and the places where we do make contact, very few cameramen would be able to walk with all of the garbage they have to carry. But tell him to keep watching the television anyway. In this war anything can happen. Usually, the areas we work in is about waist deep in mud and water. Sometimes it is over our heads. A lot of the area is filled with booby traps which are really treacherous. My platoon hasn't lost any men since I have been with them but one of our other platoons lost seven men (wounded) about a month ago and another company in the battalion had three killed and many wounded yesterday. Bad news.

Not much has been happening around here lately but we are moving this next week and should begin to catch some good action. I hope so.

I'd best go now and get some work done. Take care of your selves and tell everyone I said "HI"!

Your Old soldier boy cousin,
Ed

November 23, 1968

Letter to Ed's Aunt Dorothy Johnson

Dear Dottie,

Hi Kiddo. You really had me stymied. I got your letter, but until today, I did not know your address. You never put a return address on it, you stinker! But today I got the cookies; (I could not wait until Christmas to open it). They were really good! By the way, thanks for the sympathy card; it really wasn't meant when I said it.

I got a card from Pat, Roger and the kids, but lost their address, so I am enclosing it in your letter. Please give it to her. I also got a "care package" from one of the Johnstown, Pa. junior high schools and it was a pleasant surprise.

Nothing much has been happening around here lately, except last night a unit about two miles from us got ambushed and had 7 people killed. That was a bad scene. We were on alert all night. We've not had anyone in the platoon injured yet so we have been pretty lucky. It isn't bad here at all. I've got a place to sleep, food to eat and a dirty river to wash in; can't ask for much more.

It must be cold at home now, probably snowing. Here it is the beginning of the dry season and is about 95-100 degrees during the day and should be getting much hotter. How's that for something to look forward too?

I'd better go now and see how the platoon is getting along. Take care and be good. I'll see you when I get home next year.

Love,

Ed

Ed Dull

November 14, 1968

Dear Dad,

I'm sorry I have not written sooner, but we've been moving and being a ready reaction force always doing something. Until today I have barely had time to sleep.

Really, I've not had much more information on what I'm doing than what I have written before. We moved last week and ran a few sweeps and put out platoon and squad size patrols, but haven't had too much action. My platoon got probed the other night but we got illumination and sprayed the area with M-79 (grenade launcher) rounds so nobody got inside. Didn't get any body count out of it; they are hard to claim once you kill them. The tide washes the bodies out and their buddies drag them away for burial.

About the feet; they are a lot stronger than those of a lot of my men. They aren't giving me any trouble at all now. The only problem I have is the same as everybody in an infantry unit in Vietnam; that is jungle rot and ringworm. The jungle rot (and crotch rot), (bad news)) are pretty well cleared up with the dry season, but the ringworm is all over my ankles. I asked Suzie Blades if her dad, Carl, the druggist, had anything for it since the medics here have put out stuff that doesn't quite finish it off. If you could go pay Carl what I owe him, if he has something for this problem, and send it to me, I would appreciate it.

I don't think I'll have much trouble now. This place is work but it is also a little bit fun. I do get homesick for the States and you all, but I am usually too busy to think much about it.

I guess that is about all for now. Take care of Mom and yourself. Tell Bobbie and Jim hi for me when you see them.

Thank you for the interest in the Coal and Coke Field. I wish we could have drilled the deep test wells while we still had it. I know there is another field under there. I guess we will find out for sure soon. Keep me informed on how it is coming.

Love,
Ed

November 1968

Dear Dad and Mom,

Just a note to send along with some pictures I took a long time ago.

Not any news to speak about. Frankie says you two are talking quite a bit now. Don't give away any trade secrets of mine! OK?

That's about all. I am having a great time on my extended vacation! See you all in September!

Love,

Ed

Ed Dull

November, 1968

Dear Dad and Mom,

They say, no news is good news but no news does not fill up sheets of writing paper and that is not good news for the people back home. Am I correct?

I got the cookies and food stuffs from you the other day. They were devoured by myself and one other guy within an hour.

I am usually pretty good about sharing things, but when it comes to food, forget it! I've become a stingy old man. They were great!!

I'm working now alongside a guy I went to school with at Murray State. He graduated in January before I did, from ROTC. We ran around together a little bit there but now it's like old friends. We've been filling each other on what happened to all of the old mutual acquaintances.

Have been getting letters from almost everybody. Got one today from Dr. and Mrs. Lumbattis, my dentist. Also, one from Imogene Bleeks and of course every day from Frankie, she is really a sweet girl.

I got a letter from Bobbie that said my niece Donna got a black eye and was showing it around like a champ! Sounds like a Dull!

I'd better sign off now and write some other letters and tell them war is not always Hell. Today it was boring! Be good and take care of each other. OK?

Love,

Ed

November, 1968

Dear Dad and Mom,

Nothing much happening now, but Saigon got rocketed last night. Pretty close to our area of operation. Tomorrow we've got a good operation. Should be fun. Got a birthday present from Bobbie and Jim. Also, one from Suzie Blades and from the Jack Crouch family. That was really nice of them to think of me after all they have been through after Jack died.

Other than that, I worked on my birthday. Nothing new around here. I got your letter and appreciated it very much. Take care of each other and don't make too many typing errors while typing those letters for Dad's business!!

Love,

Ed

P.S.

No action on patrol yesterday. It was just a tromp through the boondocks. Was in mud and water up to my waist most of the time and a couple of times over my head. Got a good bath anyway, if that is much help. Not much happening now. I hope President Johnson's bombing halt of North Vietnam works. The south Vietnamese are not too pleased with it.

Gotta go now and get some sleep. It's late and I am tired. By the way, I am sending Suzie Blades a couple of things. She'll be giving them to you later. It is just stuff I have picked up on operations. Bye now.

Love,

Ed

THANKS!

THE BEST DAMN INFANTRY BATTALION

IN THE UNITED STATES ARMY
APPRECIATES YOUR SUPPORT
5th Battalion, 12th United States Infantry
" WARRIORS "

Ed and Vietnamese boy on bridge Saigon

Men working on blast wall

TA Riggins, Sgt Rush and Plamundon

Me, Sgt. Pruitt, two of our men

CHAPTER 6

DECEMBER

December was hot and dry. The monsoons had quit and the rice paddies were drying up. This was a blessing for the soldiers on patrols. We began conducting cloverleafs with more speed while still avoiding travelling the dikes between the rice paddies. The dikes were notorious for housing boobie traps.

We went on sorties called eagle flights by the companies. The purpose was to swiftly go into an area where the enemy was suspected to be located. The senior officers in Battalion S-3 (operations officers), using their intelligence received, would target a village. We would load up six men per Hughey helicopter until each platoon was on board. Then we would swoop to the edge of the suspected village and jump out each side of the helicopter while it was a couple of feet above the rice paddy, form up and conduct sweeps in the form of a cloverleaf until the village was secure or the enemy was encountered and engaged. In most cases this was an exercise in futility without encountering the enemy.

On one such Eagle flight, upon seeing the target village, I received word that we were coming into a HOT LZ. This meant that the enemy had been spotted and were firing in our direction. I alerted my men to be prepared to hit the deck as soon as possible and the helicopters would be slowing down above the paddies but not staying in one spot for any length of time so they did not pose a large target. My heart was racing and adrenaline was pumping! As we dropped down to below treetop height, I felt stinging on my face and heard firing as loud as possible. Explosions going off. I believed I had been hit by gunfire. I looked over from my position at the door with my feet on the skids of the helicopter to my left to see the door gunner grinning! He had been firing and the empty hot fired casings had been hitting me in the cheek. We then jumped out of the helicopter on the fly with them barely slowing down and formed up for the sweep. The mission resulted in none of my men being wounded and we did secure the village.

We then moved from the rubber plantation firebase to secure the alternate brigade Base called the Fishnet Factory. Since Saigon was a port city, this had been a factory where they made fishnets. It appeared to be a walled citadel. I believe it was on the highway between Saigon and the Ben Luc Bridge. The Fishnet Factory was a supply and administrative office of the Brigade. The fortifications were on both sides of the main highway in and out of Saigon. This road had constant traffic all day and evening until curfew each day. Many of the people who worked in Saigon travelled this road in both private vehicles and public transportation, such as brightly colored and overloaded busses.

Duty at the Fishnet Factory was good since we received two meals each day that were hot meals prepared in the main kitchen and delivered to each of our units for chow times. We could eat on paper plates with plastic forks and knives. Good living! We still lived in the hooches, but it was more secure than being in the field. One evening I had gotten my plate of hot food. I went to my hooch and sat on top of the sandbags enjoying the dry weather, eating the warm food. Since it was evening the busses full of Saigon workers passed like race cars jockeying for position at the Indy 500. One of the busses was loaded with the workers ready to be home for the night. Three local dogs ran across the highway and as the bus skidded to a halt, only one of the dogs made it to the other side. The other two were carnage on the road. The bus skidded to a halt and both the side door and the rear door of the bus flew open. People were shouting on the bus as a person flew out of each door heading toward each of the still animals. Each one grabbed a dog and ran back toward the bus, throwing it ahead of them as they remounted and the bus got underway. People on the bus cheered and the mood was very exciting. They were going to have a good meal tonight!

For me, I just took the plate and threw its contents into the trash barrel by the road. Even though I had been given a prized hot meal, my appetite was gone with the death and awareness of the future of the two former dogs. This brought a very clear awareness of the difference in the cultures of home and this very foreign country.

Normally, platoon leaders for line platoons were rotated to keep them fresh. I had been in the field and with the first platoon for almost four months by December. Rumor had it that my replacement was in country and should be in the field to relieve me by the middle of the month. He was a first lieutenant who had been a special forces officer. His name was Carey Walker. The waiting game was on!

Close to the third week of December I found out that Carey would not be in the field for another couple of weeks. He had been at BMB in the evening. The base had strung up sheets and played movies in the open air for the soldiers. During the showing of the movies, BMB came under a rocket attack from one of the villages near the base. The Viet Cong had fired 122mm rockets that were very powerful and deadly. After the first salvo landed, Carey ran toward the bunkers that were placed to protect from such attacks. As he neared the bunker, it received a direct hit from one of the 122's. A number of men in the bunker were injured. Fortunately, he had not quite arrived but went down on his knees to stop and skidded on the gravel tearing up his knees and sending him to the doc for treatment. It would be later before he would arrive to become the new platoon leader. Hugh Foster, then our company XO, who had been watching the movie with Carey, took off in the opposite direction hoping to outrun the rockets and ran full tilt into a clothesline and nearly was decapitated.

George Sheridan, the second platoon leader and I wondered about the fortunes of war. We were in the field where the action was supposed to be happening. The new guy was at Brigade Main Base, a supposed safe area, yet, it was at that time more dangerous than the field.

Our company was at the Fishnet Factory on Christmas Eve. The United States Government and the North Vietnamese had entered into a 48-hour cease fire to be observed during the Christmas eve day and Christmas day. By cease fire, the word we had received was that we would conduct our operations as usual during the cease fire, but we would not initiate firing or other hostile actions during this time. Basically, we said it was just a free peek from each side as to the locations and armaments of the opposing side.

On Christmas Eve I sent out my squad sized patrols as usual with strict instructions they were not to fire under any circumstances unless the other side fired first. Dumb, but necessary unless someone wanted to trigger an international incident that would not have a good ending for anyone on our side that was involved. One of the medics, who had been a conscientious objector due to his Seventh Day Adventist Religion, asked to go on the patrol to see what one was like. I let him go. Later the next month he would die in a firefight while tending the wounded. His father asked if he was carrying a weapon and we said no, he was not. That relieved the family somewhat.

The evening before Christmas was calm and starry. Even though it was a cease fire, we still had the sentries and security surrounding the compound at peak efficiency. All of us remembered that Tet the prior year was also a religious holiday. Some people do not keep their word during a war!

I checked each position surrounding our platoon area and made sure the sentries were awake and alert. I sat on top of one of the bunkers with one of my men, Private King. In the conversation I found out he was from Bartow, Florida. A good friend of mine, a girl I had dated in high school, had moved there while in high school. King said he had been to her wedding a couple of years before. Wow! Half a world away and we had a common friend!

As we sat on that hooch, in the distance we could hear and see Snoopy, the DC 3 that normally carried a set of 5.56 machine guns that rained bullets like a dog whizzing in the sky. Maybe the cease fire had been dropped and we were back in action? Then, we saw red, green and white flares dropping to the ground like mini-Christmas balls of light from the old warbird. What a pleasant change. Not death, just a celebration of light!

When my watch shift had been relieved by the next duty officer, I went to my hooch. The day before I had received a care package from Doctor Jim Setzkorn and his wife Jane, from Mt. Vernon, Illinois, my home town. Jim must have contributed to filling it. He inserted a Playboy Magazine, a small 1-ounce bottle of Kahlua and a small Christmas tree candle. Jane had put canned ham, crackers and cookies and other goodies to fill it out. That night I splurged and covered the windows of my hooch and lit the Christmas candle. Sipped the Kahlua and read the Playboy by flashlight, thinking about what the family was doing back home. This was my first Christmas away from family, as it was for many of my men. I was alive, my men were in good shape and for tonight nobody was shooting at us.

Each of the soldiers looked forward to care packages from home. It meant that people back home did actually care about us. The boxes might be small or large, it was the thought that counted. We had shortages of medical supplies including treatment for jungle rot and bamboo impetigo. There were no supplies that treated this in the Army's bag of tricks. From home, Carl and Mary Blades had the Walgreens store. They went to the different doctors in town and collected all of the samples of Tinactin (then a prescribed topical for skin disease. They sent these to me at various times. I gave them to our medic to use for the skin problems on both the jungle rot and the impetigo. It was so much better than was available through our medical supply chain. Also, a friend from home, Jack Crouch had died in 1967 in Vietnam. His mother sent me a care package. It broke my heart to know that even though she had lost a son in this vicious war, she was reaching out to make other soldiers feel the love from home. There were so many others who helped give us a little piece of home through these packages. We could never thank them enough.

Christmas passed without incident. On the 29th we received word that our Battalion, the 5th of the 12th was being taken into Brigade Main Base for Stand Down. This was the first stand down since I had been in country. I was not aware of the term or what it meant. My Battalion Commander said that it was a time to regroup.

We packed all of our gear and trucked North to Long Bihn motoring into the Main Base like the wagon trains on the prairies. We went to the 5th of the 12th area at BMB and set up. The officers were able to stay in the wooden barracks and eat at the Brigade Mess Halls. The enlisted went to their areas. It was great to be able to take a real shower and use clean bathrooms. Even going to the central piss tubes was nice. Haircuts and clean uniforms were mandatory since we were now in the presence of the main command. Who knew who would visit our units?

We also found out that inspections were being made and equipment was inventoried, replaced and weapons were worked on for the future.

Not only was it a rest for our men, but also a time to prepare for what was to come in the future.

I remember on New Year's Eve I was at the Brigade Officers' Club. I found two other officers I had been with at Murray State or Officer's Basic at Benning. It was nice to see familiar faces who were doing well. It was very nice to be clean from base showers, well fed from the Officers' mess, and going to bed in the wooden bunkhouses with raised floor and metal cots with an air mattress. Not a worry about setting out patrols, going on patrols or changing guard.

Ed Dull

December, 1968

Letter to the Carl Blades family

Dear Mary, Carl Suzie and Skip,

Thank you so much for the Christmas goody box. That was really something else!

I couldn't believe it had all those things in it! The cigars and candy I know for a fact were good! I have started them already. I didn't think you would remember about the cigars though. The rest of the goodies are going to be saved for a couple of days, I hope.

Things around here are quite calm. I am now the mortar platoon leader and in quite a bit safer position. I still will be in the field with the line platoon men, but don't have to do the sweeps and all the walking. Now, I will be directing the mortars to support the line platoons. It is quite a bit of fun. In a couple of months, I will be going back as an executive officer of the company, I hope. That is where life is easy. Swimming pool and all that good junk.

I know this is short but I really don't have a lot of time to write and wanted to get this mailed ASAP so I'd better sign off. Take care and have a very Merry Christmas. I will be thinking of you all! Thank you again for the goody box.

Love,

Ed

December 7, 1968

Dear Dad,

This is not a whole lot, but just a little bit to say Happy Birthday and Merry Christmas. I got the box and appreciate it so much! With all the stuff for my feet I won't be able to walk. Who cares? My poor feet need that! Also, thank you for the cigars! They are good for chewing!

We are on the move now. We are pulling up stakes and going north somewhere. I will find out where tonight. We will probably be there until after the big offensive against us, probably sometime after Christmas.

I will write more later. Give regards to everyone back home. Wait until Clarence drills around the #2 well on the Coal and Coke to see what he gets?

I've gotta go now and get ready to move. Take care of yourself and Mom.

Love,

Ed

Ed Dull

December 15, 1968

Dear Mom,

  Merry Christmas! This is not much, but I know you like paintings. These are the real things. They were painted by a Vietnamese and peddled out in the boondocks. I thought you might like to hang them somewhere. They are painted on Silk so they should not crack. I hope you tell me how they came through the mail. I hope they make it ok. Have a Merry Christmas, and drink a toast to me. I will be drinking a toast of Kahlua that was given to me by Jim and Jane Setzkorn, to each of you. Tell Bobbie and Jim hi for me. Also, Wielt Mamma.

  I am having a great time here. I have lost weight and look like a thin human being again, not pudgy Ed. After all, the only reason I came here was for dietary purposes! The tape player is great. How about sending some batteries and another tape or two would be great! Maybe one by Sergio Mendez and Brazil 66. Ok?

  Gotta go now. Beaucoup work to do. My love and Seasons greetings!

Love,
Ed

December 2, 1968

Letter to Dr. Jim and Jane Setzkorn

Dear Jim and Jane,

Its late and this is being written by flashlight so please excuse the misspellings and sloppy writing. I received your goody package yesterday and have been out on a search and clear since this morning at 6. I had to organize it last night so have not had much time to write until now. I couldn't believe it! That was a Class "A" (or as they say here "Numbah One") bachelor pack, all the way from the Playboy Magazine to the bottle of Kalua for Christmas Eve. That will be my toast to the people back home, OK? The cookies did not last too long. I'm afraid they were too good especially. I really can't say especially since it was all great! The oysters and sardines, I am saving them for a couple of days just got to make some if it last for a while. The handy wipes and Kleenex are strictly Waldorf Astoria type of luxury around here. They are handy but very rare. It is a change to wash in something like the handy wipes, since my baths are all taken in the local river which serves all the rice paddies and everything else in the area. Half the time I am about as dirty after bathing as before. That's the breaks. It's not quite the Bel Aire East, is it?

A little fill in on what I do around here. We are a line rifle company now situated south of Saigon. It is near a place called Nha Be, a small village. We have three separate platoon positions, mine being way out in the boondocks. We either run patrols (day and night) within the platoon or go on company sweeps, (tromping through the rice paddies for a few miles); or cordon and search (get up at about 2 am) and circle a village to keep people from leaving while the Vietnamese National Police search it for VC. Sometimes we take off for a few days and go out to an area called the "Pineapple Grove" and meet Charlie (VC) on his own ground. It usually hurts us more than him but you can't win all the time, especially in this game.

Right now, in the time we are not on operations, we are building our defensive positions for the Offensive expected in the next few weeks. That is of prime importance. So, the men are working hard at it. They should. Their lives will depend on it. I guess that is the best incentive a person could have for doing a good job!

Being here has a funny effect on you sometimes. The things you take for granted in the States are luxuries here. Things like riding in a car, taking a bath or a shower in hot clean water. Also, little things like today in the middle of our operation it was about 100 degrees out here and I got to thinking *about how good it would feel to be back in the states swimming in a nice clean pool. Then I thought how impossible that would be since it is about 35 degrees in Illinois right about now!!*

Well, that's about all for now. I've got a meeting with the other platoon leaders in a few minutes. Again, thank you both for all the goodies. It was most thoughtful of you both! Take care and have a Happy Holiday season.

Best Wishes,

Ed

Christmas Eve, 1968

Dear Mom and Dad,

You crazy wonderful people! You sent so many packages that I don't have enough room for all of them. The tape player is great. The tapes are great. The goody box was fantastic and now the box with the socks, the goodies and the game are something else! Really, you both are the greatest things since lollipops!!

Tonight, is Christmas Eve and it is quite a bit different from being at home. It's hot, not cold. I'm in a hut of sandbags with a roof 4 and a half feet high instead of a warm home and our Christmas tree is not much to look at, it is about 2 feet tall and has 4 ornaments on it. Our colored Christmas lights are flares of red, white and green dropped by a DC-8 affectionately called Snoopy. It is not at all like being back in the states with Christmas cheer and jolly people laughing and running around saying "Merry Christmas"! to everyone they see. Rather, here it is a day of respect for our Lord. It is a day that we give thanks each in his own way, that we are alive and after we finish our job here, we will go back to a country where we have the ability to freely worship God along with the other freedoms which we have always taken for granted back in the World. Yet, which must be fought for and sacrifices must be given in order to obtain them.

Maybe a little eye opener was meant for me to look into the real meaning of so many things I've always taken for granted.

This is short for a letter, but I've got to get some sleep so I can get up early for work tomorrow (Christmas Day). Take care of each other. I love you both more than you know.

Love, Ed

Officers billets BMB

Me, just returned from search and destroy

Hooches being built at firebase Libby

CHAPTER 7

JANUARY 1969

All good things must end. Such was the Stand Down and our time at Brigade Main Base. We motored out to one of the firebases along the river. I had brought Carey Walker, my new replacement so he could go on missions with me before taking over the first platoon. He was a very capable platoon leader.

I then took over the weapons platoon. This consisted of three 81-millimeter mortars. Along with the weapons was the fire direction group. The weapons went with the company and would be set up to cover the infantry movements with fire. Each round weighed about 9 pounds. They consisted of high explosive rounds that exploded on contact with the ground, or the white phosphorous rounds that were used for marking where the rounds would hit by exploding and sending white explosion that could be seen to mark where the future shells would land. We called them spotter rounds. The white phosphorous was still very dangerous and would burn anyone or thing it came in contact with. My platoon was seasoned and I was very fortunate to have a Sergeant, I believe Sanchez, who had been in the field for a few months and was excellent on fire direction.

The fire direction was key to a good weapons platoon. North South stakes were placed to sight the weapons. The tubes swiveled on a heavy metal base. The distance was determined by pulling off a number of bags of gunpowder that circled the base of each shell and by adjusting the angle of the mortar tube. The type of explosion for either ground contact explosion or deep impact was determined by turning the fuse on the front of the mortar shell. The gunner would site the barrel and its height, the other gunner would pull the bags of powder off the shell, adjust the fuse and insert the shell in the top of the tube. When given the command he would drop the shell, it would ignite the propellant in the tube and be sent to its target, for a distance of up to 4300 meters from the mortar pit. In daylight it was a challenge. At night it was extremely difficult to be deadly accurate. This was the heaviest close in support for the line platoons.

We would have a number of preset target locations for each day and night. It was coordinated with the line platoons so we did not fire into their ambushes or patrol locations. It was also designed to be a deterrent to the Viet Cong who travelled their routes at night. Many of the night targets were on the canals that traversed our areas.

On the night of January 11th, we were firing the preset target locations. We had a secondary explosion which meant we had ignited something from the enemy. The next day George Sheridan's platoon did a cloverleaf in the area of the explosion. His men found a major enemy arms cache consisting of mines, RPG rounds and shells of various types. On the 20th he again found a large cache that consisted of 56 AK 47s and 22 SKS rifles. These were on the riverbank and were in small boats that had been sunk in shallow waters and covered with plastic to keep the weapons and materials dry. I was able to take photos of these weapons seizures.

January 4, 1969

Dear Dad and Mom,

    Hi Folks! Happy New Year!

    This past year has really been something else, hasn't it? Bobby's had another wee one and I've gone for a long vacation on one of those far away tropical paradise islands where they guarantee plenty of sunshine and exercise! (Watch the small print on those travel posters, they can be deceptive!) Really, though, the year has been good to us. No real harm has come to the family and if all goes well then next year, we'll all be there to celebrate these holidays again.

    This New Year was really pleasant for me because after being out in the good old Pineapple Fields (two times without getting any men from the company wounded). Then for four days we went back to Brigade Main Base at Long Binh for a three day Stand Down beginning New Year's Eve. We all got cleaned up and I went to the Officers club for a few drinks and a great New Year's Eve party! We're now back in the field near Bien Chuan guarding another bridge. I won't sweat that.

    New Year's Eve was really funny. Sitting at the Officers Club bar were three Murray State graduates from my class. Also, there were two other guys from Fort Benning Officers Basic that I knew. It was like a couple of class reunions.

    I hope you both had a good holiday. Again, I am sorry I couldn't be with you both, but as you know it could not be helped! (They didn't mention personal servitude as being part of those extended exotic island retreats)!

    Take care and God be with you both through the coming year.

Love,

Ed

Ed Dull

January, 1989

Dear Dad and Mom,

It was good to hear from you again. I liked your client, Frank Pilcher's letter to you. It was very witty. I liked how he stepped on the airline stewardess's foot so he could meet her. Then he wound up marrying her.

Nothing much has happened here lately, except got the hell mortared out of us the other day. It was really great! We got about 40 rounds inside our perimeter and really blew the stuffings out of everything! It was more fun than the 4th of July, but was a little bit scary at times.

About you all coming to Saigon or around here, I would not advise it. You would be more susceptible to being injured than would a soldier. These people don't appreciate round eyed civilians in the least. This is my job so I'm here but no use in inviting trouble. Also, with my job I don't think I could get away for more than a few hours. We can never tell what is going to happen. Also, I could be in an isolated area where I couldn't get away at all such is the case now.

That is really great about Bobbie and Jim being able to go to Florida for vacation. Mr. Alberding sems to help out our vacation planning since he owns the Fort Lauderdale Beach Club Hotel. I would like to go there when I get back home. They might not let me come back after that vacation though. Too wild.

I will send you some pictures next time I take some. I don't get to take them that often now. Just now got a few pictures with the Polaroid, that are enclosed. One is of my platoon Sergeant and one is of the squad working on top of the bunker. The last is of me in front of the number 2 mortar of our platoon. I will send more when I get them.

I'd best be going now. Take care and be good. See you in 7 ½ months!

Love,

Ed

P.S. Notice the new white socks in the photo? I do need them too!

Letter to Bill Cox, close friend of Ed and Marty Cox's older brother.

January 18, 1969

Dear Billy,

Well Preacher, Congratulation I heard you are going to be ordained tomorrow night. That is really good! Wish I could be there with you all and see you but my vacation was extended here because of all the beautiful scenery and I won't be going home for about seven more months.

Really, this place is not too bad if you like to be on duty all of the time, live in mud and eat with the flies and bugs all of the time. This place is better than Texas. The mosquitoes are larger, the rats are bigger, the grass higher and more people carry sidearms. The cats here don't chase rats, it is the other way around, and the rats usually win. The mosquito repellant seems to attract the insects rather than keeping them away from us.

Really, the country is a mixture between beautiful and ugly; rich and poor; very old and very new. You can walk through overgrown rice and pineapple fields so thick you cannot see two feet in front of you and then out of nowhere you stumble onto a statue of the Virgin Mary all overgrown yet dominating the scene. Or you can go to a battle-scarred firebase and find it located in the middle of a once beautiful Buddhist Temple or old mansion. It is sad to see the children who have to steal in order to eat and have no regrets about it because it is the only way of life they have ever known. You have some chocolate and give it to one kid and if he is the biggest, he might be able to eat it if his mother doesn't take it away and sell it to someone else.

As you know, I am partial t young women (as usual). I am really amazed at some of these girls. Hey are so beautiful as children yet by the time they are eighteen or nineteen they won't smile and become very bitter. It is such a waste that these children must grow up the way they do, seeing nothing but reality at its worst and learning to accept it and become part of it in order to survive.

They sell everything to the G.I. and feel justified about it since we are paid such an enormous sum of money (usually a hundred dollars or less is what we keep here in country every month). The Vietnamese refuse to believe the G.I can be broke since he receives a high steady salary and they take him for all he is worth! Yet, seeing all this, is sort of like a walk on the wild side. It makes one appreciate what we have back in the States, no matter how little is may be. We are very lucky back in the world where you can get a job, we can go to and from there without the fear of getting killed and we don't have to *worry about starting up a car and having it explode. Little things like that, life really, and the ability to go to sleep at night and expect to wake up the next morning are quite relaxing. It is odd, things we value so much back in the States mean so little here. All we need money for here is pleasure and that is very seldom, so there is little or no need for it. The five-day work week is nonexistent, over here is it is seven days a week, twenty-four hours a day if we are to stay alive. Cars are not shiny or new if they are around. Here, the only vehicles we have are jeeps for long trips (ten or twenty miles) and a few people and trucks for longer distances and lots of personnel and equipment. Really, cars are only pipe dreams.*

The funniest thing is life itself. Back in the world it is everything. Here, you see people die or get maimed and then it is over. It doesn't mean that much. In order to keep functioning properly, it can't mean much, otherwise, nobody would venture to do anything, even their own job. It is really a change of standards, a one hundred percent change. That is a couple of reasons why it is so hard for a person going back to the states to adjust to living in a good society. The depth of the effects will be different on each person, but some scars will be left, it is just that way.

I think I have found the right girl at last. I'll find out when I get back to the world. She is sweet, cute, kind understanding, smart and faithful. To top it off, she can cook. Now who could ask for anything more than that? Could it be that Old Ed is finally beginning to settle down and take things as they come? The only thing I am worried about is if she will still have me when I come back? One thing in my favor is that she didn't really know me very well before I came here so she won't be too alarmed at the way I have changed. We will see then.

Well, I guess this has been long enough for a chapter of a book. I hope it hasn't been too boring. Write when you have a chance and take care. Tell Pam and your folks "Hi" for me. See you in about seven months.

Best Wishes,
Sailor Mouth Ed

Dear Dad and Mom,

Hi folks! Nothing much is happening here except our second platoon, George Sheridan's, came up today with the largest cache of weapons this battalion has found! It had 54 AK 47s and 24 SKS Kalishnakoff rifles. One of the pictures is of that cache and the other is of a cache found the other day. A bunch of mines, rockets and clothes and bandages were in a sampan. I've got some junk from another cache and if possible, will send it home. It is a carrying case and adjuster for a rocket launcher captured this past week. It is pretty cool. It will make an ok souvenir.

I am having a great time. Plenty of sunshine, fresh air and exercise and many beautiful and interesting sights that are not on any guided tours. Things such as bunker complexes, real first-hand seats to a live firefight utilizing anything from rifles to gunships. Yes, as the Colt 45 malt liquor commercial says, "It's a truly unique experience". (Pen ran out of ink, got a new one) This is where you say "wish you were here" to someone you really do not like.

On the pictures I sent, see if Suzie Blades wants to take them to school with her. They may be interested, maybe not. Ask her opinion.

Well, I hope Bobbie and Jim have a good time in Florida. They should. It will be one of the few times they will have alone without any kids.

Well, got to go now. Take care and don't worry about me. I'm having a good time.

Love, Ed

Ed Dull

January 26, 1969

Dear Dad and Mom,

Nothing much happening here this week. I enjoy the war more each quiet day. It is the best war I've been in lately. It is picking up quite a bit around here. About two days ago we helped get 41 VC bodies through artillery fire and all that good stuff. I think they were heading our way with bad intentions on their minds. Good thing we stopped them. I think the Tet Offensive will be starting any time if Mr. Charles can get his stuff gathered up and if he has enough stuff to attack. We've been doing a really good job down here. I think we've hurt Mr. Charles quite a bit in the past couple of weeks. It is good but it has been hard on the whole battalion's nerves and in loss of personnel.

Today a stupid mistake happened. D Company was waiting on a river bank for extraction from an ambush position and U.S. Navy boats come toward their position. They signaled to the boats but the Navy mistook them for VC. Navy opened up with everything they had. The Navy is not known for their accuracy with weapons, Thank God, and they only wounded four people. But they screwed up a perfectly good day for "D" Company. It is pretty bad when you have to fight for survival against fellow Americans. Kind of seems like the situation back home in the States, doesn't it?

I will probably be going on an in-country R&R in the next month or so to Vung Tau. It is a resort city on the coast of the China Sea. I sure could use it! Do you realize I have wrinkles? Must be getting old.

Dad, how is my money situation coming along? Has my Corvair been sold yet? I sure would like to get it off my hands before I get home. I can't see a person my age owning two cars; at least until I get married and that would be quite a while away. If I could get a statement on how my bank account is coming along, I would appreciate it quite a bit.

Well, I'd better go now and get some rest now. It is quite late and I need some sleep for work tomorrow. Take care and God bless you both!

Love,

Ed

P.S. Sorry about the rumpled condition of this letter but it sat under my sleeping mat until I could find an envelope. PSS made contact and killed eighteen VC in the Pineapple. It lasted three and a half days. We lost three choppers and five Americans. Not bad but we know we killed many more than eighteen. Things are picking up.

VC cache, January 16, 1969 - George's platoon

Weapons cache. January 20, 1969

Me on patrol with mortar round

Sgt. Mike Gross on patrol

Me sitting on mortar emplacement

Fire direction control hooch

Mortar firing, FSB Kathy

CHAPTER 8

FEBRUARY AND MARCH

The rest of January and the first part of February was peppered with small contacts with the enemy. In 1968 before I arrived, the TET offensive began on January 30th, 1968 and went for a couple of months through the country of Vietnam. We were on high alert starting toward the end of January of 1969 that there would be a repeat of this offensive for the current year. Our Battalion was moved to a river bank west of the Saigon area to prepare for a massing of Vietcong or North Vietnamese regulars. We were in an area about five miles south of Duc Hoa in the Pineapple area. Our company also protected a group of Navy fast boats that were located on the river. One evening, one of the Navy ensigns came to our camp and invited my men to sample an animal they had killed and were cooking over an open fire. It was an alligator. They had cut the tail and were having an old-fashioned barbeque. This was the first time I had eaten alligator tail. We talked about white and dark meat at home, but this was pure white. Not bad and tons better than c-rations!!

I was in charge of a weapons platoon at that time. This consisted of three 81 mm mortars. I had them set up in a cemetery since it had flat land and was higher than most of the land surrounding it. We had coordinated our tubes with where the infantry platoons had set up lines of defense through the area. My preset targets were in a protective area around the different platoon locations. Each of the platoon leaders had received word that the Viet Cong were massing for an attack in the next couple of days. We all were on high alert.

At approximately 1 am I received word that Lt. Carey Walker was on the horn. I checked with him. Carey said he was on a hill top about a thousand meters from my post. He was concealed and could hear movement below him. He wanted mortar fire to his front. I asked him exactly where and he gave me coordinates where he needed the fire. My platoon sergeant set the tube and we fired a round. Carey said to keep firing. We fired six rounds. Shortly afterwards Carey said he could hear movement closer to his position, between where the mortars had landed and his hill top. We fired another round of three. They were closer but he still wanted them closer. I asked him how close those rounds had been to his position?

He said they were about 30 meters from his location. He did not want to fire on the enemy himself. That would give away his position and would compromise our company location. I told him I could not fire closer to him since the mortars are not pinpoint accurate. He still wanted them closer. We split the difference and fired another salvo of three. It was right on target and there was no more noise. The rounds were about 15 meters from his defense line. Due to his heroic actions our company line of defense was not disclosed. The next morning, he located bodies of Viet Cong below his position. This was very important since the next day all hell broke loose in our area.

I was asleep midmorning. I had been sleeping on an above ground burial casket since the water table made digging impractical. This was a shelter with open sides and a roof to protect the granite slab on which the casket laid. I kept thinking flies were buzzing around me. It was very annoying and was bothering my sleep. After I woke up, I realized the flies were bullets striking the granite of the various tombs in the cemetery. The battle was on about a three or four hundred meters to my front. We became active and started firing in support of the line platoons who were in direct combat with a regimental force of Viet Cong.

The battle lasted most of the day. When it was over, we had four soldiers wounded and no fatalities. We had killed 24 Viet Cong and captured two other soldiers, according to the after-action reports. We had also recovered weapons and one NVA radio which was great for intelligence purposes. My old platoon, with Carey Walker at the helm had performed flawlessly. One of the Viet Cong who had perished was found to have a wad of ganga, a boiled chewing gum like substance narcotic in his mouth. Maybe they needed that false sense of courage to be involved in such a charge.

When the battle was over and we had regrouped, we were redeployed to Fire Support Base Kathy. This was a two-company fire support base. C company was on one side of the canal and D company was on the other side. After we were in place and settled into a routine of daily patrols and sweeps, I was offered a three-day R&R in country to Vung Tau. This would be my first break from duty in over six months and I was taking it. I had to take a jeep to brigade Main base to get cleaned up and then take a series of small planes to fly into this beautiful city by the South China Sea.

Vung Tau was a recreation area for all of the Allied troops. It is located on the east side of Vietnam approximately 100 miles east of Saigon. The city is protected by mountains separating the airfield from the western edge of the city. The city is a colonial seaport that borders the South China Sea and has the most spectacular sugar white sand beaches in the Middle East.

As I arrived from the airport by bus, we were deposited at the

Officers' barracks, a two-story building guarded by soldiers with M-14 rifles. This is the only time I had seen these rifles in Southeast Asia. I inspected one of the guards who was dressed smartly in his pressed and starched uniform. When I asked him about how many rounds he carried, he replied "We are not allowed any rounds in the weapons, only in the ammo pouches. There is a concern we might discharge it and create bad relations with the townspeople." That thought was not very comforting as I went about the rest and relaxation.

The next visit was the Officers club. Totally a beachside affair. Then a change into swimming trunks and going to the beach. Although the beach was beautiful, there was still a war going on and rolls of barbed concertina wire were separating the areas where soldiers were allowed. Young Vietnamese girls came on to the beach with Coca Cola and other drinks. Some of the girls also had pineapples that they would cut the outer layer and sell to eat like a large popsicle. Unfortunately, if you ate the spine parts your mouth would become numb. Yes, fresh fruit, no, unless you learned how to eat it!

There were warning signs about the heat and the sunshine. If you became sunburned that was ok. If your sunburn caused you to not be able to return to the war zone and fully function, that was an Article 15 offense. That was similar to a mini court martial. From the waist up not a problem since we had been in the sun for the past six months. From the waist down yes, a problem. Care was needed to either wear some sunburn cream or wear long pants.

The skyline of the city along the sea was gorgeous. The rumor was that many of the US hotel companies had purchased property here and would build major hotels after the war was won by the Americans against the horrible communists. Supposedly Howard Hughes, Hugh Hefner and Marriott lost these investments when that did not happen.

After the beach a number of us went into the town to the local bars.

Since this was a seaport, there was a mix of soldiers, merchant marine sailors and civilian Vietnamese. There was always a question of whether Vung Tau was the R&R location for the Viet Cong as well as our troops. Then home to the Officers barracks that were guarded by soldiers with rifles and no shells in the chambers.

The R&R was supposed to be three days and two nights. About three the next morning the airfield and a number of buildings and fuel tanks were rocketed. The airfield was a couple of miles from our barracks, but we still heard the commotion. We were rounded up and the next morning were placed back at the airfield and sent back to the war. This was only the second time during the war that Vung Tau was targeted. Just my luck. Plus, my rest and relaxation were cut short one full day. At that point the firebase was quieter than the rest area.

Back to Fire Support base Kathy. I was in charge of the fourth platoon, (weapons platoon). Then the third platoon leader rotated back to the states, so I also was in charge of the third platoon. These guys were for the most part seasoned soldiers who had shipped over with the battalion the previous June and some replacements.

One of the guys, a sergeant, had been in country for a while. Since things were not very active and we were close to Saigon, he went in to the city on a day pass with the meal truck. He was supposed to return late in the afternoon with the evening food truck. He did not show. No word why he did not come back. I could not get any word on the radio to company headquarters or battalion. Late the next day, I received word he would be out in the field the next day after a couple of nights in the brig at Brigade HQ. When he did appear, it was without one of his stripes, now officially a specialist 4th class.

Sarge had been to a couple of bars on Tudo Street in Saigon drinking the Ba Mui Ba (33) Beer. He decided that he needed to take a peddle bicycle trip around Saigon. This was a bicycle with a wide seat on the front of the bike. When the trip was finished and the peddler asked for payment, Sarge realized he was without funds. Rather than asking another soldier for a loan he panicked and started to run. The peddler enlisted his friends, the other peddlers to assist in the chase. At the front was a lone, somewhat inebriated soldier, followed by an array of angry and very vocal peddlers and Sarge was losing the race. He spied a local bus idling on the side of the road. It's driver, having no passengers had stepped away to get a soda. Sarge borrowed the bus and put it in gear. Now, the peddlers were accompanied by the bus driver and the local police all in behind the bus. Sarge, looking for a friendly face saw a group of US soldiers at a gate in downtown Saigon. He pulled in to the gate and said," Take me, I am yours!" It was the gate to the US Embassy. They did, straight to jail. Our lowly sergeant almost single handedly caused an international incident in downtown Saigon.

Rather than put him in jail, the military reduced his rank, paid the peddler an amount for the bus ride by taking money from his pay and sent him back in the field. Yes, he was contrite, but he was also a hero in the company from then on.

The nights in our area consisted of ambushes and the days of patrols. The brass believed we needed to be more aggressive in our practices. One way this could be accomplished was to conduct a platoon size roving night ambush. My platoon, third platoon, was selected for this task.

The plan was to start like each other ambush. We would go to a point just before dark and settle in, like this was our destination. Then after dark we would move to the ambush point some 50 to 100 meters in a different direction. This was ok since we had done this many times before. After about an hour or two, we would then move to a second location about a kilometer away. We would stay here for a few hours then move to a third and final ambush site and stay until dawn.

The concept was well conceived, the action left much to be desired. The Vietnamese were very familiar with the dike systems and the rice paddies. Although the Spring monsoons were not yet in full force, we would be wading through streams and dike systems in the dark and it was starting to be muddy. The moon was not full so it was very dark This action was not the best thought out that had been conceived.

The first phase went as planned; no contact was made so on to the second phase. We set up as an L shaped ambush on two dikes that were about 3 to 4 feet high and in a muddy rice paddy. The men were spread out in good order. The ambush was set and we were where we were supposed to be on the map. About two in the morning, we received word from battalion that a South Vietnamese artillery unit was going to fire 105 howitzers over our position, but the target was about a kilometer to our front. Not to worry, we were not in any danger, it was friendly fire.

The first barrage went over us and hit on target. A short time later, I heard what I believed was a girl who I had known and had been dating, screaming at the top of her lungs. Startled, I yelled for the men to hit the deck. We all dove into the muddy rice field off of the dike. Just as we hit the water, a short round from that barrage hit on the other side of the dike, peppering the top of the dike where we had been just seconds before. I heard one of the men yell. It was Mike Gross, one of the replacements. I checked for injuries. There were none. When Mike dove into the paddy, a snake went down the top of his uniform shirt and slid down and out the bottom of the shirt.

I checked with battalion telling them about the short round. The Vietnamese checked their fire. No more shells came through that night. We went to the third location without further incident and after daylight went back to camp. Then I wrote an incident report. We did not have any further roving night ambushes after that. The Vietnamese were familiar enough with the terrain to move freely at night, we were not.

I wrote a letter that day to Francine, the girl whom I heard scream. I explained that we were not hurt and because of her warning we were all safe. Mail took one week to go each way. So, one week after I sent the letter, I had received one from Francine. (She had not received my letter yet and would not for another week). Francine said she had been at work in Toronto, Ontario and had become ill in the afternoon, about one or two. She believed that I had been hurt and she had to go home from work. She was concerned about my safety and hoped everything was ok. This was the same time I had heard the scream. That letter sent chills up and down my spine. Yes, there is a God and he does work in mysterious ways! It was not until a couple of weeks later that we got settled down.

The village near Fire Support Base Kathy was hostile. It was reputed to be a VC stronghold. We did not interact with the villagers and they reciprocated. Late one night a rocket hit the corner guard post of the unit on the other side of the canal. It killed at least one soldier. The platoon leader of that unit, Jim Davis, tried to save the people in that bunker. Within a couple of hours, both our company and the one across the canal mounted up and surrounded the village while it was still dark. The action was called a cordon. The object was not to let anyone in or out of the village until the Vietnamese police and ARVN (Army Republic of Vietnam) could go through each hooch (hut) and arrest any people deemed to be Viet Cong or sympathizers.

It was dark when we mounted up and formed the platoon in squad sized lines to advance on the village. Helicopter and jets were called in to support us. The jets dropped some ordnance in front of our advance. There were two Cobra gunships that were circling as well. In the dark the Cobras must have mistaken our platoon for enemy. They fired rockets at us. They landed short but put us on the defense rather than being able to advance. After relaying to our command, they were called off and not seen again. Communication is the key and, in this case, as well as others it was lacking. We stayed at that cordon for a full day with no good results.

Later that month we again were sent on an eagle flight that became a large village cordon. This was a joint effort of our company and other companies. My platoon was the end of our company and joined with another unit which was not on the same radio frequency. This made communications very complicated. I would radio to my company radio net; they would relay it to the other unit and so forth. My unit ended at a deep creek about one hundred feet from the other unit. We placed flares in the creek between the two units to prevent the enemy from creeping between us.

At dusk we heard movement in the creek between us and the other platoon. Snap! One of the trip flares went, the next one exploded. The other platoon started firing into the creek area. Unfortunately, we were directly in their line of fire. Then their machine gunners started firing directly into us. I tried to yell to them to cease fire and also was contacting my company commander to tell them to check fire. After what seemed like an eternity, probably about five minutes of fire, we checked the creek and had successfully killed two water buffalo who had gone to the creek for evening watering. Each platoon adjusted our lines of fire and had no further problems.

The next day, Mike Gross had an encounter with one of the villagers. Private Gross, who later was promoted to sergeant, was on guard of the main road into the town. A woman went toward the village from the outside. Nobody was to go in or to leave without authority. Mike challenged her and she would not stop. He was concerned she might be a bomber or VC sapper carrying explosives. We did not have an interpreter so it was a guessing game. Finally, in a universal language, she lifted up her shirt showing she was a nursemaid for village children and she needed to be with her wards in the village. He let her pass.

Later that night all was quiet or so we thought. When a person needed to complete their personal hygiene, we would go outside the wire if there was no latrine available. One of the men went out after letting the men on perimeter know where he was going. Not more than a few feet in front and to the side of the 90 mm recoilless rifle. The 90 mm was the modern stepchild of the bazooka. It fired a shell that was an exploding, high impact round, or as was the case that night, a fleshette round which contained thousands of small steel darts. As the soldier was squatting, a trip flare in front of the recoilless rifle went off and the recoilless rifleman immediately fired at the flare light. The squatter was far enough to the side of the rifle that he did not get hit by the backblast, but immediately sat down, ruining the moment, his mood and clothing as well.

The fleshettes did their magic though. This time it was not a water buffalo, rather a couple of Viet Cong who had been sneaking out of the village. They were found the next morning when it became light.

We finished the cordon and went back to the Firebase.

Ed Dull

February 2, 1969

Dear Dad and Mom,

I got the food yesterday and the socks. Thank you, it was really good. Out in the field we could not get boxes and heavy stuff because of weight problems. We have to carry what we receive. But now, at the firebase we are loaded down it seems.

We aren't doing much now except building up for the big offensive. In the next day or so we will be moving again. This time probably north of Bien Hoa toward the Cu Chi area. Should be fun.

It was surprising that your friends, Mr. Mateer and Mr. Farrar sold all of their interests in your wells. Have you decided if you will sell your interests as well? If so, which ones will you sell? Will I keep my interest in the Manahan well?

I got the can of popcorn from the Mateers! It was very good but did not last any time at all around my guys.

I will go on an in-country R&R to Vung Tau. Think I will sleep the whole time. Can't think of anything better to do.

Not much of anything more to say right now. Take care, see you in seven months.

Love,

Ed

February 12, 1969

Dear Dad and Mom,

I'm going on R&R on February 21-28 to Australia. It sure will be a needed break. I was going to Hong Kong but this one was at hand so I decided to take it. It should be quite a rest. I really need it.

Lately we've been firing about 500 rounds from our mortars a day in order to get my crew a little practice in firing. In about a month over half of my platoon will return to the States so I'll have to get a new bunch of gunners. That will be my main trouble. So that is what we are doing, training new gunners. We're working them in 3 shifts 24 hours a day and I don't get a whole lot of sleep because I'm supposed to be up and with the guns when they fire. But we are not getting any return fire from Charlie, so he must be steering clear of our area. After we leave this area, it should be desolate all around here. That will suit me fine!!

I have my doubts about going to Australia this next week. I'm liable to get there and not want to come back here. That happens you know. It'll be odd to walk in a city street and see a blonde, red head and tall brunettes. Also, to not have to look at people who are trying to blow you up. To be able to walk in fields that are not full of mud knee deep and still have dust blow in your face. To not have the air desecrated by the smoke of weapons. It will definitely be a change for the better. To be able to eat food that does not give you dysentery and be able to sit down for that meal and take your time about eating it. It is something to look forward to at least. I'll send you some pictures of it and some post cards while I am there.

I hope this new well you are drilling turns out pretty good. Every year is a new one and this one should be exceptionally good. What with the year being the return of Ed. Guess Who? Mom, I know your book review will turn out good. You are always good at speaking. Your main trouble is worrying about the little things. But I guess worrying is one of the prerogatives of women!

I might go back to school next year if everything goes right. I've still got to send in applications and all that stuff. I might not leave here in time to start the Fall semester. We'll see.

If you can please send me my book "Masters of Political Thought". It is on my bookshelf in my bedroom. It is a paperback. Also, if you can send me the book on great court decisions. That is another paperback in the same place.

By the way, tell Doctor Jean Modert that if he had contacted me a couple of weeks sooner, I could have sent him about a dozen AK 47 magazines plus an AK 47 web belt for magazines used by Charlie himself. Also, an AK 47 oil can for oiling the weapon. But, since we have to carry everything with us, I couldn't keep toting it around the countryside. If I can get any off some of the caches or otherwise (I am not buying them, that is not fair according to Hoyle) then I'll keep if he will send a money order to cover the cost of shipping it. It may be a while since we've had little contact lately, but then again Tet starts this week, soooo.

Put in your request for war trophies and I will see what I can do. Unless the superior officers take them, I may get a weapon for myself, ones we have captured, an SKS (AK 47s can't be sent to the US any more. Even blocked and welded. They are all going to US Army posts for training aids or to troops here to be used for the LRRPS (long range recon patrols) to use in order to draw less attention when initial contact is made. It confuses Charlie. (Ask Sam Mateer about that. He knows since he just got back home).

Well, not too much more to say other than I'll drop you a line when I'm in blissful, bullet free country of Australia! Take care.

Love,
Ed

Feb. 14, 1969

Dear Dad,

I got your letter a minute ago and really feel good about you selling my car. Now I will have a clear conscience about spending all that money in Australia. We are in the middle of a move to a new location today and everything is packed so this will have to suffice for now as writing paper (this letter was written on the back of a bank statement I had just received).

Tet offensive should start in a couple of days, (maybe today or tomorrow), so until I get to Australia my writing may be sporadic. We are moving toward Long Binh, our Brigade HQ today, to an area I have never been before. It is supposed to be called V.C. Hill. I hope it is named that because of its looks and not because of any action that has taken place there. But I am probably wrong! Thank God I will only be there for four days until I have to go back to Main Base and process for R&R. Hate to say it, but R&R will consist of little except round eyed women, sleeping and party time! I

I do wish this month would hurry up and end. It will probably be my luck that the real heavy fighting will begin the day I am scheduled for leave on R&R! Then I will have to stay here and fight instead of enjoying myself.

I am looking forward to meeting Dave Berry upon my return to the world. He sounds like a pretty smart character. Maybe I can get a few ideas from him about going in the law field. Also, maybe he can help me get into law school. I will need all the help I can get.

I hope your new Rehn Hudson well turns out good. That would be quite a break for us all. To tell you the truth, you say Mom does not sleep very well at night. Neither do I. I will probably be pretty jumpy for a while after I get back home. Get prepared for it.

Take care of yourself and Mom. I have not gotten the box from Marshall Fields but should pretty soon. Should be yummy! So, thank you in advance.

Love,

Ed

Ed Dull

February 17, 1969

Dear Dad and Mom,

I won't be going to Australia. Too much of a chance we'll get hit this next week. Can't win them all.

We moved again on the 15th up to an area north of Saigon and south of Long Binh. We are east of Highway 316. We are now set up in a temple area right in the middle of their grave yard. I hope it doesn't cause any hard feelings with the Vietnamese since this is their Tet Holiday. Some of the enclosed pictures are of this area. Some others were taken at Fire Support Base Kathy in the Pineapple Fields last week. Since we have been here, we haven't fired anything since we are under a cease fire until tonight at six o'clock. We are in about a ten thousand meter long and five-thousand-meter-wide area of operations now for our company. We raised so much trouble with the Battalion in the past couple of weeks and cut them down so many times that they divorced our company from the rest of the Battalion for a few weeks. They put us in our own separate area of operations directly under Brigade control. This place is really great and there is supposed to be a good enemy force in this area. I'm looking forward to a little contact in the near future.

After my in-country R&R in March, I'm getting a new job. I'm getting tired of being a platoon leader and after six months we're supposed to be able to get out of the field. I've got my eye on one MACV (Military Assistance Command Vietnam) job that looks pretty good. I don't want to stay in this battalion much longer. It is so screwed up that around here that it is not very safe. The coordination is bad on the battalion staff and logistically the light infantry concept as they are using it is quite inadequate. I think I should get a nice desk job and just sit back and let someone else get shot at for a few months. The fighting isn't bad. My company is the best, but the harassment by the confused people upstairs is something else. So much for that.

Did you have a good time at Bobbie's house? How is their family? Good, I hope. Hope this winter at home hasn't been too bad. The winter here has been really hot and dry. It rained a few weeks ago, but not enough to even settle the dust. The rains should not come again for another six or seven weeks.

That's about all I have to say right now. Not much more except that enclosed is a letter of information about the Tet holidays. Just a little information. Also, the pictures; please save for when I get home. See you all.

Love,

Ed

February 20, 1969

Dear Dad and Mom,

I am, as you can tell, still in sunny South Vietnam. I picked up the money on the 18th from Red Cross and put it in the company safe. Sorry to cause you all that trouble and expectation. Maybe, I can use it sometime later since I cannot do so in Australia.

The way you talk about the new farm you bought sounds great! I remember looking at it once before I left. I think that was before you bought it. I will be glad to help you fix it up when I come home. We'll also have a place to hunt next fall. Make sure you get the guns registered this year. What are you planning to put on it? Cattle more than likely. Doesn't it have a house on the property? What kind is it and what shape is it in? Maybe I can stay there for a while when I am home. Maybe I'll buy a horse when I get home and keep it out there. (I'll feed it all the time since I will be home; not like Tony, my old horse you had to feed when I was at college!). Maybe I could stay around there for part of the winter and go to school at Carbondale for some extra courses. But that is to be seen when I come home.

We are going to move again back to the Pineapple Fields. Really don't too much want to go there, but don't have too much choice. I am really getting tired of moving around so much. I'm going to try to get into Saigon pretty soon and see about that other job, but I want to wait until after R&R in order to take it. I need the rest; my wrinkles are getting deeper. I'm beginning to look like a 23-year-old man. But that should go away with some rest.

I guess I had better go for now. I have quite a bit of work to do. We've really built quite a lot since we have been here. Too bad we have to leave so soon. Take care of each other and God Bless you both.

Love,

Ed

Ed Dull

March 1, 1969

Dear Dad,

It happened the other night. Wouldn't you know we'd still be here in the Long Binh area too? They have one VC regiment about six miles to my south that came through the eastern sector of our AO (area of operations). And hit Long Binh. We got some of them with our mortars but not a whole lot. (They bypassed us; we were not important enough to hit). Twenty of them penetrated the wire around Long Binh about one o'clock on the 23rd about an hour after they rocketed and mortared the Post. There were five GIs killed and 89 wounded. About 150 VC were killed. The next day, my company swept east of our position and killed 6 and captured 3 VC. We had 3 wounded, only one halfway bad (in the arm, he goes home). That night we fired some rounds to support elements around here and killed a few more. Yesterday, just sniper fire and yesterday afternoon, the rest of the company was ambushed in a river boat (LCM8 Mike Boat) and wounded 3 more of our men. None were seriously hurt. My platoon was not there.

Last night my platoon fired 65 rounds on enemy movement. I haven't got any word on how many we killed.

So far, our company has captured 6 AK 47s, 1 M-16, 1 AK 50 machine gun and a new VC radio. We also got a bunch of ammo, web gear and magazines. I've got 1 AK magazine for Dr. Jean and one for myself an oil can (VC) and sweat rag taken off one of the bodies. Most of the stuff (web gear etc.) is pretty gory with flesh and bone particles stuck to it. Can't win them all.

Enclosed is the picture of the cache taken off the bodies my company got. Should be quite a bit more to come. My platoon area is supposed to have been hit for the last two nights but have been lucky so far and just got a few sniper rounds outside the perimeter. I think we could have held off most anything and come out ahead though. This place is in the last picture I took and has a trench system all inside it. We have about 45 claymore mines out all around the perimeter which is 170 meters long and 50 meters wide. We have 3 separate lines of concertina wire (triple strand) set a maximum 50 meters from the perimeter and machine guns and 90-millimeter recoilless rifles covering the likely points of approach. I'd like to be here if we were hit.

I'll be sending this junk and other stuff home as soon as I can get some packing material. You take care now, because I am sure I am! Hope you and Mom had a good time in Hawaii.

Love,
Ed

March, 1969

Dear Dad and Mom,

I just got to read your letter that had Susan's wedding article in it. How did Dad's checkup turn out? Good, I hope.

Nothing much is happening around here. We have been on a cordon of a good-sized village around here. There were eleven companies involved and we circled their village. Then we began to close in tighter and check all of the people in the village. Now, some more companies have been added and we are still here.

We have been here five days and so far, killed ten VC and captured eleven more.

My platoon has been in one good firefight so far. It was really cool! Bullets going everywhere, hand grenades going off, the whole works! We might have killed three VC, but are not sure.

I should be going to Battalion by next week for a new job. Hope so.

So, my niece Shelley is learning how to walk! That is really great! I can't wait to see Bobbie's kids when I get home. I bet they will have grown a lot!

I had better go now. I hope Dad's checkup came out all right. Write when you have a chance. Take care of each other.

Love,
Ed

March, 1969

Marty Cox, a family friend who is a senior in high school
Dear Marty,

It is really great to get your letter and quite a surprise also. I want to thank you for the letter and the support you all are giving me over here.

A war is a funny thing. All of us over here are one thing. Black, white or other, we are soldiers. The men I work with are from every type of life; gamblers, thieves, hoods, college graduates, high school dropouts. Loud mouths and quiet people intermingle all for one purpose; to fight for our country. The majority of them are draftees, people who did not want to be in the army at all, much less, 8,000 miles away from home to live a dirty, risky life for a year in Vietnam. Even while they are here, they are not afraid to tell you they don't want to be here. But, once these men begin to work, whether it is filling sand bags or going out on a sweep in the rice paddies where there might be quite a few who won't come back, these men are soldiers fighting for our country! Just GI's doing what is expected of them. In 12 months, those who are left will go home to the States. They will once again become the same gamblers, thieves, gang leaders or whatever they left. Back there they are what they will be, but here they are the same people with the same purpose. They need the support of the Americans who have sent them here to protect the future of our Nation. What the people back home do for these people will have an effect on these people for the rest of their lives. If they know someone is thinking of them over here, they will do their jobs with an easier conscience and possibly do a better job to support our country once they return to it.

Marty, all these people are real, for I have them all in my platoon. Some come to me and boast; some cry on my shoulder; some gripe, but behind it all, they just want to be supported if they do their jobs.

The most shocking thing I saw was on my first day in the field. We had a man, a medic, who was griping about his job. He kept saying that he was humping the paddies all the time for what??? He was underpaid, underfed and if he was hit who would care? Nobody cared. Hell, half the country doesn't even support the war. The next day we were on a sweep and we heard two loud explosions fairly close together and knew the other platoon had hit booby traps. They brought the wounded to our area to be picked up by medevac choppers. Among the wounded and one of the worst hit was Doc Townsend, the one I had been listening to the night before. Later, I found out that even though he had been wounded very bad, Doc had told the others how to patch up the others, whether to give them morphine and other help with his buddies. Doc is a soldier, the same as the rest of us. He, like the rest of us need assurance and faith. That's where you all come in helpful. Every little thing the people back in the States can do to let us know that you are behind us helps us more than you would know.

Thank you, Marty, for writing and God Bless you this coming year.

Best wishes,

Ed

Letter to Susie Blades, Mary and Carl's high school daughter

March 20, 1969

Dear Susie Q

Hi there to the best looking girl in Mt. Vernon! How might you be today? I hope you are feeling good because I am in a way, but in a way not.

My unit has really been stomped on this past month. My company is the only one that hasn't been really torn up; we haven't had anyone killed and only two wounded really bad. We have had a dozen or so minor wounds. Yesterday was a bad day. I found out a guy I was with at Fort Benning and also Fort Leonard Wood was killed a couple of weeks ago. He just tried to do his job and never finished it. He was a good guy; we were all together on New Year's Eve. Another kid I that I used to run around an awful lot was hit a couple of days ago but will be all right eventually. He was going to Hawaii in a couple of weeks to get married. That is what hurts.

This is an awful thing to talk about but I have to tell someone. I can write about two things; one is reality, the other is dreams. Reality is here and all I can do is tell it like it is and that is not really pretty. It does not often become happy but it is all true and out there. It is meeting people one day and never seeing them again. It is a child who talked with you one evening and later finding out her village was attacked and always wondering if she lived or died and never being able to find out. That part is reality.

Then there is the part of dreams. Dreams about going home and not worrying about staying alive. Being able to be in a quiet place and enjoying it. Being able to go where I want, when I wish without having to carry a weapon. It will be great to have the whole world open to me when I get back. That might be reality someday, but for now it is just a dream.

Maybe the world right now isn't so bad though. I got my teeth checked at the Fishnet Factory today and found that I don't have any cavities. Happiness is having thirty-one teeth (I got one pulled last year), and all in good shape. Maybe that is not

Snoopy's way of putting it, but it will have to do for now.

I think about you a lot Susie. I think about what you were like when I left and wonder what you will be like when I come home. I think about how crazy you are at times like when I came to the drug store with my college girlfriend. You ran up the aisle gave me a big hug and said to her "It's alright, we're getting married!" That was something else. I don't think I will ever forget that! Other times it is other things I remember. I only wish there was more to remember. It seems that I have known you for so long yet know you so little. Strange, isn't it?

Maybe I have said enough for now. Maybe, enough for quite a while. But that is me. Please take care and study hard. God Bless you, Susie.

Love,
Ed

Ed Dull

March, 1969

Dear Dad and Mom,

Just got back from my 3-day R&R in Vung Tau and had a great time. It was the rest that I've needed for quite some time. It is a nice town about 70 miles east of Saigon, located right on the South China Sea. It is surrounded by water on three sides and a mountain on the fourth side. It was almost like being out of Vietnam completely.

I just swam in the ocean, ate good food, drank good wine and slept in an air-conditioned room in a real bed with sheets and covers and all those things. We had running water that was hot and cold and even flush toilets. It was really living like a king! I appreciated that more than most anything. For the first time in almost seven months, I was actually clean!!

It seems like Mt. Vernon has really changed quite a bit in the past seven months. I guess progress can't afford to be stopped. It will look quite nice though. But I think the best addition to the town is your farm! That is what I want to see.

Not much more to say now, so I will sign off for a while. Write you soon.

Love,
Ed

March, 1969

Dear Dad,

I really appreciated your letter. I did not realize it had been quite a while since I had written. After Vung Tau, I had a lot of catching up to do in work. We got a rocket inside the perimeter night before last. It scared the hell out of everyone. We thought we were being hit by a ground attack, but nothing else materialized and nobody was wounded. All is well, I guess. The other company in the same firebase killed six VC about 500 meters from our perimeter today. Old Charles was trying to sneak by and didn't quite make it. We're at a new firebase right on the edge of the Pineapple Fields and it is pretty active around here. We should be able to get some action around here before we leave.

I don't know when I'll be changing jobs now. I have not had a chance to go to Saigon and see what is up for grabs. I should be changing soon though. I've been in the field for over six months now and that is just about rotation time. Haven't had a chance to get to Saigon to see my high school friend Stuart Webb with the MPs yet either.

That farm of yours sounds better all the time. Not only is there lots of room, there is also a good fishing pond from the way you talk. Looks like I might be quite a nature lover and farmer when I get home.

Enclosed is the division order for the oil interest. Thank you for sending it. Speaking of money, how about sending me a copy of my bank balance. It should be about even now, with the withdrawal for R&R. By that I mean the same as the last balance you sent to me.

I guess that's about all going on around here for now. Take care of you and Mom. See you in five months.

Love,

Ed

Eagle flight landing at firebase

Interrogating VC prisoner

Mike Boat resupply with jeep

CHAPTER 9

APRIL

During April, we continued the regular process of sweeps, patrols, and ambushes at night. Bathing was not regular. Because of the limited clean water and prioritizing it's use for cooking, brushing teeth and shaving, the use for showers was limited. It was required that each person would shave daily and brush teeth. Normally, there was a two wheeled container of non-potable water that could only be used for cleaning, washing clothes and showers. This was refilled on an as needed basis. The showers we made consisted of an enclosed area with a single shower on raised slats and no roof. Showers were limited to a bag made of canvas with a rotating head that could be screwed one way to increase the flow of water and the other to stop the flow. I believe it held one or two gallons of water. The goal was to get in wet down, stop the flow, soap up all over then turn on and rinse quickly. If you ran out with soap still on the skin, it could cause infections. The soap we used was sterile military disinfectant soap. The use of shampoo was discouraged. The use of after shave lotions was prohibited since the scent would give away our positions while on ambushes and when in the field. Normally, we would bathe once a week when we were in base camp. In the field it was not at all. The running joke was on ambushes late at night, one of the guys would turn to another and say" you stink!"

The back and forth. Of course, we all stank!! Smoking during ambushes was also prohibited. The light from the match or lighter and the smoke and smell was a great target.

The outhouses at the firebases usually consisted of a building with two or three holes set in a row. The need for privacy was replaced by the need to use the facility. Under the holes was a 55-gallon drum cut in half. This was changed daily due to sanitary content as well as the smell. This was a tropical climate, after all. Cleaning the waste from these containers was known as the "shit burning detail!" It was not a sought-after chore. Usually, it was reserved for the person who needed a refresher course in doing things right. The cleaning method was to take kerosene, soaking the contents and burning it until it could be scooped out. When we had extra pouches of mortar propellant, that could be added to the mix to make it hotter, burning quicker. At the times that a firebase also had 105 Howitzers, the extra charges could be added to the mix. On those occasions the smell of the burning waste was not as bad due to the extreme heat of the fires. All part of housekeeping under primitive conditions. Good health and sanitation practices meant the people would not become ill.

On April 17th, 1069, my platoon sergeant, Kenneth Bull was scheduled for a night ambush. We had discussed it during the day. Kenny did not want to go that evening. His concern was that he had just 31 days left in country. I had told him that once he got back in the morning, we would make some changes to get him some relief from being in the field. I knew he had at least two great soldiers with him. Carl Green, at one time a sergeant, and Larry Lauzon had both been in the field for a long time and were seasoned soldiers. I knew the patrol would be in good hands.

At approximately 2 am I heard a small explosion, like that from a grenade. About 30 seconds later, a huge explosion. Then quiet. I got on the radio trying to find out where it came from. I Checked patrols and could not raise the ambush team. All other patrols and ambushes and outposts sounded off except for Kenny's ambush team. I contacted the company commander about sending out a team to check on them. He refused to let me send one out due to the possibility of being ambushed.

After almost an hour, we were radioed from the ambush team that the VC had set off a large homemade claymore mine aimed at them and had killed a number of the team. I asked if they were secure and was told they were. We sent a medevac chopper to their location to evacuate the dead and wounded. Once that was complete, they returned to base and we got the after-action report.

What had happened was that Kenny had decided it was safer for the squad to enter an abandoned hooch for the night instead of laying the ambush. The VC, finding this out, set up a homemade claymore mine consisting of a 55-gallon drum base filled with explosives, concrete and metal shards aimed at the front of the hooch. The hooch only had one entry or exit point. Then the VC set off a grenade a little distance off of the hooch. Once the men exited through the front of the hooch outside, the VC set off the claymore hitting a number of them going through the doorway of the hooch. Kenny Bull, Larry Lauzon, and William Smith were killed immediately. Carl Green died at the hospital due to the wounds. Each of these men were great soldiers. All of us were devastated at their loss. Although a number of my men were injured or wounded, these were the only men in my command who were killed while in Vietnam. The loss of these men was tragic for each of us in the company. I am sure their families felt a tremendous loss. They were all good soldiers, friends and brothers to us all.

Ed Dull

April, 1969

Dear Mr. and Mrs. Lewis,

It is quite a pleasure to hear from our Sunday dining partners. From the way you talk, there are quite a few new restaurants at home now. Maybe you will join us when I get home!

Mom wrote something about Mr. Lewis ending his job as City Manager, but did not mention his working for The First Bank. That sounds like a good job.

There is not too much to be said for this place except the cost of living is very cheap compared to the U.S. But, out in the rice paddies and swamps there is not much chance to buy anything. It is quiet here compared to last month about this same time. I would appreciate it if the place would stay quiet for a while also.

Not really too much to say except I hope you had a happy Easter. See you in about five months!

Sincerely,

Ed

April, 1969

Dear Dad and Mom,

Happy Anniversary, a little late!

Sorry I did not write sooner but have been quite busy the past week or so. We have been on another long cordon around a village and after that, moved our company base to a different location. Now we're located at Rinh Chanh, and the facilities are really nice. Clean water to wash in and nice buildings to live in. It is really too much! And to top it off, it is easy to get to Saigon from here. So, maybe I'll get to go in sometime soon.

I finally got an R&R. I'll be taking it in June to Hawaii instead of Australia. Imagine a week of charming American girls and eating hot dogs and drinking American beer!!How's that for living? I might like it so much that I won't bother going back to Vietnam. (Impossible but we can always dream). It was the only R&R that was open, so I decided to take it. I would have rather gone to Australia but at least this is being away from VN.

Not really much more to say. I hope that your new well, the Rehn Hudson turned out all right! The picture and the newspaper article look quite impressive.

Take care and God Bless you both!

Love,

Ed

Mike Boat resupply Mekong

Our kit carson scout and two of my men

Platoon size patrol

Sgt. Mike Gross

Chapter 10

May

We moved from that firebase back to Na Be and the Fishnet factory shortly after that time. I stayed with the third platoon and I believe another lieutenant took over the mortar platoon. Although the Fishnet Factory was larger than the firebase, it seemed less hostile. This was possibly since the people nearby were city workers from the Saigon area who travelled the road daily to and from work. When there were hostilities, their daily work patterns were disrupted and commerce, goods and work stopped.

When we would travel in more populous areas, I noticed the protective measures around the homes. In this tropical area, air conditioning was not prevalent. The houses were two story and open to the outside air. Thin curtains would blow in the breeze and the air flowed freely through the homes. This made for good circulation, but also invited potential burglaries. The ledges surrounding the homes were lined with broken bottles cemented into the top of each outer wall. It was a permanent form of barbed wire that I had not seen before. I guess each society has its own way to protect the people.

While in this area we were deployed to guard the bridge at Ben Luc. This was a small village and a nondescript bridge crossing a small river. This reminded me of the many bridges crossing the Wabash River back home in Illinois. The same routine as when we were in Saigon guarding the bridge, but on a much smaller scale. The men would shoot any flotsam in the river and drop a small charge of TNT into the river to deter any underwater activity.

One morning I was sitting in the command bunker speaking with the platoon sergeant when there was a huge blast. A sapper was my first thought. We are under attack! Both of us jumped up and ran to the area to assess what was happening! All of the men were gathering on the bridge. The man guarding bridge said," I was just shooting at junk in the river when one of the things I shot blew up!" As it turned out, he had shot an explosive device that had been set to blow up the bridge! This was the only time the bridge shooters in our unit had saved a bridge.

The next morning, we were notified to have all the men in full uniform (meaning shirts, boots and shaved) at ten hundred hours, especially the man who had shot the explosive device. At ten hundred hours, a helicopter with the battalion commander touched down on the road. The battalion commander, Lieutenant Colonel Albert Malone, arrived, hopped out of the chopper, strode to the front of the formed-up platoon and pinned a bronze star medal on the chest of the soldier who shot the explosive device. We all saluted. Lieutenant Colonel Malone turned, got back in the chopper and then it was back to business as usual. This was a morale booster we all needed at that time.

We then rotated back to the Fishnet factory for duty. Since the Factory was the alternate Brigade base, it was common to have field grade officers in and out on a regular basis. Dress code was stricter than in the field. Uniforms had to be worn in regulation daily. No bare chests unless doing digging or lifting of supplies. It was more spit and polish than out in the field.

One of the nice parts of being at the Fishnet was eating two good meals each day. Breakfast and supper were either made on location or trucked in from Brigade Main Base. We would eat on paper plates and take the meals back to our hooches surrounding the factory to eat. Not as good as home, but better than a daily round of c rations.

Ed Dull

May 6, 1969

To Imogene Bleeks, a friend of the family

Dear Imogene,

I haven't had a whole lot of time to write letters lately. We are trying to get things ready for the rainy season as well as run our normal operations. I got the cookies and Vienna Sausages about a week ago and ate them for a couple of days. Then we moved out on a cordon of a village. So, I packed some in my duffel bag and have been chowing down them in my spare time. They are really good! You really came through with enough to feed an army, but then I guess I eat enough for an army!

I am really missing you all an awful lot, but will be back in another four months and that is now beginning to seem close. When I get home, we will all go to my grandmother, Wielt Mamma's and have chicken dinner and all the goodies like we used to before I left. How does that sound to you? It sounds like a great idea to me!

I want to thank you again for the goodies. They were really great! I am looking forward to seeing you when I get home.

Love,
Ed

May, 1969

Dear Dad and Mom,

It's late and things are going at quite a fast pace around here, so a short time for a note and some information.

My R&R will be on June 11 to June 17. I really want you to come there too. Luckily, I got to make the phone call to you. short but sweet, very rare chance through the ham operators. I take it the phone bill is something else though. It was about midnight here at the communications tent that our radio guy hooked up with the ham operator in the States. I'll send you the pertinent orders on the 29th or 30th of May. You should receive them no later than the 6th or 7th of June. That is the best I can do on short notice. I want to stay at the Ili Kai Hotel. They offer R&R rates. I will know and write you asap with that information. Please get three rooms two singles and a double for yourselves. Draw out another $400 out of my account and bring it along. I might need it.

For clothes for me, bring my blue dress suit, white dress shirt and tie to match. Bring my black loafers, good prescription sunglasses and my turtle neck blue banlon sweater. Also, bring two short sleeve button down shirts. I have one pair of brown slacks at home. Please bring them. Oh yes, a couple pairs of black socks. That should be all I need. Of all of those, I need the sunglasses the most.

Have Trish coordinate with you on clothes, transportation etc. for the trip. I will also be sending her a copy of my orders for flights, rooms, so the fare should be lower for her as well. Remember you all have priority on flights to Hawaii to visit a serviceman on R&R.

If you still have questions just let me know.

I have nothing more at this time. I will keep you updated. Take care, God Bless you both. I hope the next 14 days go by quickly. See you then.

Love,

Ed

Ed Dull

May, 1969

Dear Dad and Mom,

Hope you've received orders for the trip to Honolulu by now. A couple of corrections. I won't be going on R&R until June 12th, not the 11th. I'll book reservations for all of you at the Ili Kai on June 11th and mine on June 12th. It will be from June 12th thru the 18th. Meet me at Fort DeRussey after I out process from there.

I am now working at Battalion Headquarters so rest easy. If you have any trouble with improper forms, see the Red Cross ore the local Army recruiter for help.

See you both on June 12th.

Love,

Ed

May 25, 1969

To Suzie Blades, high school senior daughter of Mary and Carl Blades
Dear Suzie Q,

Well kiddo, I am back in the groove again. A new second lieutenant came in the other day. I took him out with me for about four operations and ambushes and turned over the third rifle platoon to him yesterday! Now I am the mortar platoon leader again. I was glad to see that guy. That platoon was jinxed. Now, at least I am not in the mud every day. That is a little bit of help.

Only about 115 days left in my island paradise and I don't think I will regret leaving it at all. The only thing I will regret will be that it took something like this to make me learn and understand so many different things. Also, it has been such a waste to have so many people, good people of all kinds, colors and religions to die for the greed of so few men. I think that I shall be very much against war when I get home. Not just this war, but all war and the damage it does to a country and all of the people who are connected to it in any way.

Just think, in about 20 days you will be a high school graduate and then soon after that it is birthday time! Wow, you are getting everything at once. You know Sue, I am proud of you. You are quite a lady!

I had best go now kiddo. Tell everyone "Hi" for me. Take care of yourself, ok? See you soon

Love,

Ed

Ed Dull

May, 1969

Dear Dad and Mom,

Sorry if you have not gotten any mail. I have written three letters to you this past month. Maybe faulty mail?

By the way, Happy Mother's Day and Happy Anniversary! Sorry if I cannot make it there. Enclosed are some pictures. I will send more as they become available. Your pictures were really good. Wish I could be there to catch some of those fish. Maybe this fall? Not much more to say. Take care and be good.

Love,
Ed

PS 2 more letters will follow with just pictures, no writing. I'm illiterate!!

Xuan Loc rock landmark

ARVN soldier with captured AK-47

Vung Tau officers club

CHAPTER 11

JUNE

During the middle of June our unit packed up and was transported to a new war zone. True to the name of Light Infantry, our Battalion moved out of the area around the Fishnet Factory, mounted on trucks and headed east to a beautiful city named Xuan Loc. Xuan Loc is on the main east route from Saigon to the South China Sea port of Vung Tau. At the entrance of the town sits a huge boulder that looks like it could fall on the road at any minute. The altitude was a little higher and the terrain was different than our prior locations. We came from rubber plantations, rice paddies and swamps around Saigon to a very dense triple canopy (three layers of trees and no sunshine) jungle.

The first night being camped around the city of Xuan Loc was peaceful. I remember the distant sound of wind chimes being hit by the evening breeze. It seemed so peaceful. Maybe this area would not be vicious like the swamps and rice paddies with their booby traps and Viet Cong who were farmers by day and fighters at night. Yes, it would be different, but not peaceful.

The next day, we moved into the jungle to virgin territory and began building Firebase Blackhorse. Bulldozers cleared jungle and a battalion firebase rose from the jungle as a short-term monument to Army building and ingenuity. Conex containers were brought in to be the bases for the command posts. Mortar and shell boxes of wood were filled with dirt and pallets for flooring were laid out along with the molded metal bridge culvert frames for the roofs of the individual hooches for the soldiers living quarters. Sandbags were filled on a regular basis as fortifications were built. Corrugated metal sheets were laid out as roofs of areas to be further covered with sandbags as overhead protection. Where yesterday was jungle, now a small fortified town of sorts was being built. One morning I laid my dopp kit with shaving supplies and toothbrush on a sandbag berm and within a few minutes it was gone. Probably part of a substructure built for one of the hooches. Within a day we were in the perimeter and within a few days it became our new home.

When we were notified of making the move there was only one day notice before we left. Our daily routine at the Fishnet was changed abruptly. While at the Fishnet, I found a Vietnamese washer woman whom we called Mamma San who took my uniforms each week and would wash and press them. She had my clothes the day of the move. I found her and said we were moving. She asked where and I would not tell her because we did not know. She said "never mind, I already know ". Off we went with me only having a couple sets of uniforms. One week later, at Firebase Blackhorse, Mamma San showed up on her motor scooter with my clothes and those of the other officers. She said" I told you I already knew where you were going!" So much for stealth and secrecy!!

Our patrols in the jungle were much different than before. Visibility was minimal, maybe a few yards to our front. The M-79 grenade launchers were not very effective since the shells could hit the jungle foliage shortly after firing and explode in front of the soldiers. This caused a change of types of rounds being used. The M-79 grenade launcher became a large shotgun with ball bearing filled rounds instead of the grenades. This was much more effective in a jungle setting.

When we went on patrols, the front men, or point persons, would be machete wielders as well. When we used the known trails in the jungle, we ran into the same problem as on the dikes of the rice paddies. Many of the trails were booby trapped with grenades set in tin cans with the pin pulled, stuffed into the tin can, a fish line filament tied to the top of the grenade and strung across the trail. When the wire was tripped, the grenade came out of the tin can and the unpinned handle flew off arming the grenade and wounding the unsuspecting soldier. So, we used the jungle area not the trails. This made for very slow and tiring patrols.

Soon after arriving we also realized why we had been moved to this area rather than the western part of the country. This jungle was a good cover for the North Vietnamese Regular Army to bring troops into the central part of South Vietnam. In short order we started to come into contact with the professional soldiers of the North Vietnamese Army.

While the Viet Cong would fire wildly and then run into the jungle, the North Vietnamese would aim for your feet, keep firing and advance. They were true professional soldiers who had been trained and knew how to fight. This was a rude awakening and our need to remember the tactics we had been taught on how to conduct warfare.

On one late night patrol and night ambush, my platoon came upon a wide smooth area in the jungle. Unsure what to make of it I asked our Kit Carson scout. The Kit Carson was a former Viet Cong soldier who changed sides and worked for the South Vietnamese as a guide. Although there was a language barrier, the Kit Carson's eyes got really wide and soon we realized a battalion or larger sized unit of North Vietnamese had just passed through this area earlier that day. I notified my commander and told him we were not moving after dark since we would possibly bump in to them. I did send out scouts who did not locate the force. We set up our ambush at that location for the night. We did not make contact with them the next day. They must have kept going the next day.

The jungle was where we also encountered a defoliant called Agent Orange. As part of Operation Ranch Hand, the Air Force sprayed the jungle to defoliate areas for better visibility. It was similar to a burnt orange thick antifreeze. The droplets would be on the leaves and splat onto the skin. We were told to try to keep it off the skin when possible but that was impossible. Little did we know it would haunt us for the rest of our lives.

Each soldier was entitled to go on a one-week R&R trip as part of the tour. The prized trip was to Australia. The chances of that trip were minimal. Some people went to Penang, Hong Kong, and other Asian destinations. I was fortunate to go to Hawaii.

The last week in June I flew into Honolulu on a military flight. My parents and a friend had agreed to meet me that week. I had not seen an American woman for almost 9 months other than nurses and donut dollies. Going from a war zone to a bright sunshine scrubbed, bustling civilian live was truly a dramatic shock. Since I had been gone overseas a new clothing fad had emerged. That of miniskirts. Women started wearing miniskirts and go-go boots during that year. Wow! What a surprise.

I met my parents and my friend Patricia at the airport. What a nice reunion! We went to the hotel, the Ili Kai for the week stay. This hotel had been made famous by Jack Lord, the original Hawaii Five O television show. Jack Lord stood on a balcony at the Ili Kai hotel looking out at the ocean on each episode.

Once we had checked in, I wanted to take a bath. That would be the first good one with constant hot water in almost three quarters of a year. I sat in the full tub, turned on the shower, popped the drain and fell asleep in the heated water. Even after that one I did not come clean. It takes a lot longer than one bath to wipe that kind of grime out of your body. My parents had brought my good suit from home. When I left for Vietnam, I weighed about 165. At the time of R&R I was about 140 or less. The suit was huge, but still was better than a uniform. We ate at the restaurant at the hotel. They said soldiers would eat the first meal free, all you can eat. After finishing off a steak, I got another one and polished it off as well. It had also been a long time without a good meal.

The week was a great respite from the war. At night when the rest of the family would go to bed, I would walk the streets of Honolulu until early morning, almost dawn. It was so nice to be able to walk without concertina wire and sentries. No limits on going inside or outside a wire barrier. The feeling of freedom was overwhelming.

It was so great being with my parents and seeing a familiar face from home in Patricia. We went to the different sights on the Island that week. Waikiki Beach, the Volcano and the beaches around the island. At night we went to a couple of shows. Don Ho, the local singer was at Duke Kahanamoku, a night club. He was famous for singing Tiny Bubbles and The Hawaiian Wedding Song. Evidently, I also saw my favorite recording person Rod McKuen of Listen to the Calm and other melodic poems. My Dad pointed that out to me the next morning. Maybe walking all night dimmed my memory or maybe a little too many tiny bubbles. Who knows? Unfortunately, the week passed too quickly and I went back through Tan Son Nhut Airbase to my unit, and to a new assignment.

June 20, 1969

Dear Dad and Mom,

I'm sorry for not having written sooner, but we've been so preoccupied in moving and setting up in our new location at Blackhorse, that about all I've had time to do is work and sleep. A lot of the former and very little of the latter I might add!

I don't know how to thank you for coming to Hawaii to see me. I know it was not easy for you both but I do hope you weren't disappointed. I was very happy to be with you even though because of my environment for the past few months I might have seemed kind of cross or unsettled.

Hawaii is very beautiful and besides just resting, it was the first family vacation we have had for quite a few years, isn't it? I think it was great! The time there will help carry me through the next couple of months. When I get home and get some rest it will be even better though.

I do hope you both had a pleasant trip back. My trip back here was all right considering the destination. I did not have you go with me to the terminal because with all the people crying and saying good bye amid the confusion of leaving it was bad enough being a detached bystander than to be a part of it. That may sound bad but the trip back was demoralizing enough. I hope you understand.

I'd better sign off now. It is kind of late and I'd better get some sleep. I have a long day in front of me.

Take care of each other and I will see you soon. Your number one son will return soon!

Love,

Ed

Building FSB Blackhorse

Eagle flight FSB Blackhorse

Setting mortar stakes at FSB Blackhorse

CHAPTER 12

JULY

Before I had gone on R&R I turned over my platoon to a new lieutenant. Now I was going to my new duty assignment at the Battalion headquarters. Maybe it would be at the Brigade Main Base in Long Bihn? I reported at that location upon arrival from the week off. The Duty Officer had my new orders cut and I went back out to fire Support Base Blackhorse. I was the new head of the forward tactical operations center at Blackhorse. Yes, I was at the front but at least I was working in a large Conex container with a group of noncommissioned officers and directing the movements of the different companies in the field from a safer location.

My job was to receive the daily briefings from the Battalion commander to the company commanders and monitor the daily movements of the units. This also included monitoring the ARVN (South Vietnamese forces) movements and other units to make sure they did not conflict with our patrols, ambushes and other actions. When the units requested firing opportunities, I would check to make sure they were not firing into friendly units or villages. Many times, it was frustrating since a platoon wanted to fire on a suspected enemy, but I could not get timely clearance for them to engage until it was too late. This seemed like too much bureaucracy at the upper levels. I was frustrated with not allowing them to engage first and ask questions later. That was part of my job though, to be a buffer between quick action and staying away from an international incident.

This part was not as easy as I had thought while out in the field as a platoon leader. My location was very good. The TOC (tactical operations center) was in the middle of the Battalion main camp, with troops guarding it, since the Battalion Commander was there regularly. My hooch was still a raised platform with shell boxes filled with dirt and topped with the bridge metal covered with sandbags. It was open ended with a sandbag berm on both sides about five feet tall to protect the ends from shrapnel going into the hooch. I was able to change into clean clothes regularly and take semi regular showers. What more could a person want? I worked twelve hours on and twelve off at the TOC and spent the rest of the time working with other soldiers making sure the area was clean, free of clutter and keeping prepared for potential attack.

During the month of July, the fighting got heavier. Most of the units in the field had made contact with the enemy and we were incurring heavy casualties. The North Vietnamese as well as their Viet Cong counterparts were stepping up the fighting.

I was working in the TOC one morning when the battalion Commander and the company commander of B company entered the TOC. They were in a tremendous argument. Bravo Company had been in extended firefights in the past few days and incurred heavy losses. The company commander was a level headed experienced commander who was not doing very well at the time. The Battalion Commander relieved him of his command right in front of me. The company commander said "What do you expect?? I have been working for the last month without two of my platoon leaders! Both had been either killed or wounded and I am running two platoons with inexperienced sergeants!"

The Battalion Commander just stared at the company commander then slowly looked around the TOC. The next words out of his mouth were," Lieutenant Dull! Pack your shit, you are going out in the field and taking over one of the first platoon of Bravo Company!"

My response was "Yes Sir!" My thought was "What in the Hell just happened here?!" I was told to catch one of the two choppers going out to the field that day. The first one left in the next hour, about 10 am. The second one, the afternoon chopper left about 2 pm. I went to the hooch to get my field items, backpack, canteen, other supplies needed. I also needed to change my personal firearm, at that time a .45 automatic pistol, for an M-16 rifle with plenty of ammunition. I also needed grenades and smoke cannisters (not cigarettes, but green and red smoke). Not only was I going to take over a line platoon, but one that was in a combat situation.

My concern was for the fact I was only a little over a month from going home. How focused would I be at this stage of my tour? So close yet so far away. So, I went to the priest who was at the Firebase. We talked for a while and he asked if I wanted him to talk to the Battalion commander? I said "No, just please say a prayer for me to do a good job".

Back to the hooch for some food supplies and to finish up the backpack.

I was bent down behind the blast wall packing the last of the supplies in the backpack when I heard a couple of sergeants talking on the other side of the blast wall. "Kind of a shame about the Lieutenant." "He was strange but not that bad of a guy". I lifted my head and asked what in the heck they were talking about?! They turned pale and both said" You are alive?"

"Of course I am, what are you talking about?" One of them said" The morning chopper got shot down as it was landing. It took an RPG to the rotor about 3 or 4 feet off the ground and fell on its side. One person was killed. The chopper fell on him and everyone thought it was you since you were supposed to be on that chopper."

It was a soldier who was running to get on the chopper as it was hit. He was going to catch it to go on R&R.

This is not a good way to enter into the combat area. I caught the afternoon chopper and was dropped into a very secured combat area next to the downed chopper. I arrived along with their food, medical and ammo supplies along with five-gallon clear plastic containers of water.

After getting off the chopper I asked the resupply guys where first platoon was located and was pointed in the right direction. When I got to the first squad of the platoon, I introduced myself and got a cool response. Another green Lieutenant who does not know anything had to be their thought.

I made it known that I had been in the field most of the past year and was not green or foolish and had their best interests at heart! This changed their attitudes right off the bat!

I asked where their leader was and they pointed to the rear and said "Sergeant Snowflake is back there"! was sure I had heard them wrong. So, I started down the line asking for their leader. Each time they responded "Sergeant Snowflake is back there somewhere." Eventually I was going down the row and saw a tall blond-haired guy running toward me. He gave me a hug. I backed up, looking at him and had to ask "Are you Sergeant Snowflake?" "Yes, I am, he said".

The name did not instill confidence in anyone much less his demeanor. He had been in Germany as a noncommissioned officer most of his career in the Army. He had been in for over ten years, but had always been in a spit and polish noncombat unit. Going to Vietnam was a totally new journey for him. He had the knowledge, but nobody to point out this was not the spit and polish Army, this was a war zone and our rules were different. Over the next few days, the men were more respectful and our ranks were more disciplined than before. It just needed a person who had combat field knowledge to help Snowflake and the rest of the platoon regain their spirit.

For the next couple of weeks, we performed very well in the field. We were involved in some skirmishes, but nothing major.

One morning, we were preparing for a resupply. It was necessary to secure a landing site that was in a field rather than jungle. The site was perfect. Just one tree at the far edge of the field. The rest was grass about four or five feet high. The company started surrounding and securing the Landing zone to make sure nothing happened to the chopper. My lead squad was to circle down to the tree. The chopper was still a few minutes off and waiting for us to give the all clear.

I heard a commotion with the first squad. A squad of Viet Cong were also at the tree. My squad leader grabbed a grenade, popped it and threw it at the VC. The Grenade hit the VC in the head and bounced off and then exploded, not hurting anyone. Then the firefight began. The resupply was called off. We started firing. We were aiming to the right of the tree since that was the only aiming point. Fire was coming at us. At this time, I thought "This is my dream!!" Is this where I die?" I moved a little to my right and threw my empty ammo clip to my left. It was hit by a bullet. "Oh crap!" "Good I moved!" We fired and advanced through the heavy grass. We were in a line with the first squad and could assess any wounded. The enemy broke off and ran. I sent a squad to track the VC and we came up with blood, a cone hat and ammo. Two of our men were wounded, neither badly.

Medevac was called in to pick up the wounded and resupply. The regular resupply ship came in later to drop off the water and supplies. I will always remember that field with the lone tree. If I had not moved, the dream would have come true.

Much of the next couple of weeks were consumed with doing sweeps in the jungle. It was the rainy season and there was no escaping the water. We could not be dry. I encouraged the men to change their boots daily and their socks as much as possible. Without changing socks, our feet could be waterlogged and get jungle rot and possibly gangrene. Even with the regular changing of socks, I could not get my feet dry. After a couple of minutes of having the dry socks on, my feet were soaked again. It was as much a battle to keep the feet taken care of as fighting the war itself.

One day as I changed my socks, the top layer of skin came off both feet and I had to leave the field. It was sickening to take off the socks and see raw skin being left behind. After talking with the medic and my company commander, I had to go back to the rear and stay a few days to let the feet heal. This consisted of working on platoon and company material, but doing it in flip flops so the feet could keep dry and covered with ointment. We got a new lieutenant and I turned over the platoon to him.

July, 1969

Dear Dad,

We are back in the firebase Blackhorse for a couple of days to rest. Didn't do too bad last week. We had two firefights last week and my platoon initiated contact both times. My platoon did not take any casualties either time from wounds. We were ready to be picked up to be choppered in to a new area and my platoon was guarding the people on the first load ready to get picked up. We saw about ten VC setting up an ambush for our last element and we opened up on them. We didn't get any bodies out of it, but we sure had fun trying. About six hours later we flushed out the same ten and had another firefight and killed a couple but so many of my men were passing out from the heat that we couldn't sweep out and pick up the bodies. That was quite a day!

The stuff is really picking up around here. It is quite a bit different from being around the Saigon area. The VC want to fight up here. Down there they fought when they were cornered. Up here they fight every time they have a chance. It is a lot more work here also because of the heavy jungle. But that is part of the job.

Well, I don't guess there's much more to say for now.

I'll probably buy a car from Belleville. I wrote to Obbie Atkinson in Mt. Vernon, and he referred me to a Mr. Holman in Belleville. It will cost a little more but at least I am sure of what I am getting.

If I can, I will take another R&R to Hong Kong. This time I will buy some things very cheap such as stereo equipment and things for the family. Also, I'll need some clothes. Got to have some things to take back to the World with me. Can't go home empty handed.

Better go now and get some work done. See you both in about 45 or so days!

Love,

Ed

Ed Dull

July, 1969

Dear Dad,

    I am wanting to buy some things for myself, Mom and you before I come home. Please draw some money out of my account or if not possible, maybe I could borrow it from you and pay you back when I get home and am able to withdraw it from the bank. I need about $300 to $400 for now and if it could be a money order that would make it easier. I would like to have it by the end of July or the first of August if possible. I might have a chance to go into Brigade Main Base and to the Cholon PX about then for a couple of days.

    We had another platoon leader come down with malaria the other day. I may wind up going to take his place. It will keep me occupied for a while. I should not be out in the field very long. Please don't expect many letters from me for a while because I will only be at the firebase every nine to twelve days, so I won't have much of a chance to write.

    Take care and keep catching those fish out at the new farm! We will have a champagne fish fry in September when I get home

    Gotta go now!

Love,
Ed

July 18, 1969

Dear Dad and Mom,

I hope all of your visitors this past week have not worn you out too much. It sounds like you both really have had a house full of people. But, knowing you, I guess you enjoyed it.

Nothing much has been happening around here. Seems like we might be in the process of lessening offensive maneuvers in South Vietnam in the near future. That would make all of us very happy since the jungle is really hurting the men by strain and physical wear and tear and disease. We've had a fever running through the Battalion that hits about five or ten men each day and takes them out of action for about 4 or 5 days. That does not help at all. Also, the foot problems are on the increase again, being in the water all the time.

But I've only got about 43 or 44 days left in country so this does not bother me too much. Like a guy once said, "I'm so short I could stand on my head and stack BBs for the rest of my tour!"

I got your letter Dad and thank you for the money. Now I can buy some things before I head home.

I'd better sign off now and get back to work. Take care and keep catching fish for the fish fry when I come home. We'll see you.

Love,
Ed

Ed Dull

July, 1969

Dear Mom and Dad,

Hi folks, I'm fine. How are you both? Have you been getting your letters from me lately? I am sorry about not writing more often but we have been working an awful lot lately and I am having trouble writing much at all.

Right now, I am mostly pushing papers here at the firebase Blackhorse. I am trying to get caught up on the records along with running the mortar platoon. They are pretty much running themselves. It's not bad now, I just hope the heavy rains wait a couple of weeks before coming. I should be going into Battalion as a liaison officer in the next couple of weeks. It will be something quite interesting and different.

I got the cookies and sausages from Imogene Bleeks and Wielt Mamma. They were really good. Those two really did not scrimp at all when they send things. It was chock full of goodies. Really good too.

Hope everything is going good for you both back home. Dad, have you got the Rehn Hudson oil well on the pump yet? I hope it turns out as a good well.

That's about all for me now. I will write again as soon as I can.

God Bless you both.

Love,

Ed

CHAPTER 13

AUGUST

After I returned to duty, I was assigned the job of liaison with an ARVN unit through the Battalion. It was a different type of assignment. Just myself and staff sergeant Sanchez, a career noncommissioned officer. We would coordinate efforts between the Vietnamese soldiers and our Brigade. It seemed strange, a small group of our soldiers working with a company or greater of the ARVN's.

The housing was good. We lived in wooden huts with concrete floors. Food was still trucked in from Brigade for at least one meal a day. The rest was C-rations or items from care packages from home.

Living among the ARVNs gave me a great appreciation of them and their daily routines. They were for the most part gentle people who had lived their whole lives through one war or another. First, being part of French Indochina, then their own nation after Dien Bien Phu. Now we, the Americans coming to say we were saving them from the evil of Communism. I believe they wanted mostly to just be left alone. The ARVNs would eventually pay the price for being aligned with the Americans.

The soldiers would show us their prizes. One had an AK-47, another would show us how they ironed clothes with an iron that was hollow and then filled with coals to keep it hot while they ironed their uniforms. For the most part this portion of my tour was uneventful.

I became aware that one of the new President Nixon's pledges was to get the US troops out of Vietnam. He stated there would be an early withdrawal of the troops that were on the ground.

First, the 25th Division was going to be withdrawn from the Central Highlands. The Division would be sent back to their permanent home of Hawaii. The orders came down that anyone who had been in the field for over nine months would have first opportunity to withdraw with them. It turns out I was eligible to go with them. I had over nine months in country and had been a line soldier. I checked with the Battalion operations on the details. Yes, I could be part of their group. The only stipulation was that, as an officer, I would need to change my status from a reserve officer with a two-year active commitment to a Voluntary Indefinite Status.

This was a commitment of five years additional active-duty minimum with a possibility of another extension after that time due to the needs of the Army, i.e., the indefinite part. I could see myself being in Hawaii for another three years as an alternative to staying in Vietnam.

On reading the fine print and talking with career officers, that was not the way it worked. Although I would be sent with the 25th and become part of their organization now, the needs of the army were paramount. I was guaranteed a rotation back to Vietnam after 13 months after going to Hawaii. After all, the war was still going very strong and there was no end in sight.

My next step, if I returned to Vietnam, would be as a line company commander since I already had line combat experience. So far, I had been very fortunate not to be wounded. Going back again would increase those odds more than anything. I decided not to accept the offer of early withdrawal and stay the last month or so until the first or second week of September.

I was notified about the 24th of August that I would be leaving early by about a couple of weeks under Nixon's early out program. A couple of weeks is a lot better than nothing at all. I was told to pack my gear and take the jeep to brigade Main Base. No complaints from me.

Upon arrival at Brigade Main Base, I met with the Brigade operations officer, received my orders and was told to get a haircut and turn in any gear I had in my possession before heading to the plane. These items accomplished I had one last night in country. I spent that evening at the Officers Club on base and ran into Jim Davis, who had been on the plane to Vietnam with me. Also, the former company commander of Bravo Company. We each gave thanks we were going home the next day. Maybe a little too much celebration was in order that evening.

The next day I was sent to Tan Son Nhut Airbase via bus. I was looking forward to that day. It was customary among the commercial airlines that the returning soldiers would receive a steak dinner on the flight home. I was looking forward to being on either a TWA or Pan American flight back to the States.

Upon arrival at the base, I was notified that due to the increase of soldiers returning home early, there were not enough commercial airlines to hold all of us. There were sixteen commercial airliners scheduled on the tarmac for the day. The government had also enlisted four C-141 Airplanes to house the overflow. Yes, I was lucky and got one of the four C-141 planes to return home. We entered from the dropdown ramp at the rear of the plane. The rows of seats faced to the rear of the plane and the windows were above the seats so there was not a view. Instead of a stewardess welcoming us aboard, an Airforce E-5 sergeant told us to take a seat. When the plane was loaded the sergeant asked who would like their steak dinner? We all raised our hands. He then proceeded to toss boxes of C- rations to us while smiling. But once the wheels came up and the nose of the plane pointed toward the sky, we all cheered anyway! Time to go home.

Next stop was Honolulu for a very short stop then back to San Francisco to out processing and catching a real commercial airline to go home.

The next day or so was a blur of scheduling flights from San Francisco to St. Louis and then home.

August, 1969

Dear Dad and Mom,

Please send me my summer green uniform, one khaki dress shirt, my black military tie and a green overseas cap. Please take them to One Hour Martinizing Cleaners and get them cleaned. Also, one pair of black socks. Do this the day you get this letter and mail them to me the next morning. Do not delay please. I will need them as soon as possible. I must have the whole uniform and be inspected one week before returning to the States. It is a Brigade ruling if one is to wear green uniforms back to the States. I'll need these clothes as soon as possible so don't delay at all. This is very important!!!! Ok?

I want to tell you that I am well and doing ok. I'm working at the battalion headquarters at the present time and getting some of the dirt out of my skin before I get home.

Looks like the VC are building up for another major offensive in the next few weeks. I hope they hold off for a while. I don't particularly want a repeat performance of Last February!

Well, I'd better sign off for now. I've got quite a bit of work. Better send the uniform by the fastest means available.

God Bless you both and take care of each other.

Love,
Ed

PS send it to me via HHC 5th BN 12th Inf 199th. The rest is the same.

Ed Dull

August, 1969

Dear Dad and Mom,

Well, each day that passes is that much closer to the day I get home again! And, you both can surely believe that I'm waiting quite impatiently!

Don't know quite what to say as not much has been happening. I haven't received a letter from either of you for about three weeks now and hope you are both in good health and have only forgotten to write or the mail has been very messed up around here. Preferably the latter.

I have not had a chance to buy anything that I wanted to before going home and probably won't be able to either. So, that kind of makes me mad. I did not buy a car because I wanted to wait until the 1970 models came out and I could get a look at them. Also, I didn't want to buy a car without at least seeing what it was like. I'll have plenty of time to look around for one when I get home anyhow.

The first week or so when I get home, I don't want a lot of people around. I just want to sleep, eat and take baths. When I want to see people, I will go see them. I don't want to be rude; I just don't want to be around a lot of people. I think you will be able to understand that.

Did Bobbie and Jim get in that bad tornado in Cincinnati last week? I hope not. It sounded like a really bad one. I heard it hit north Cincinnati so that was pretty close to their side of town. I hope they are all right.

Hope you got my clothes sent to me by now. I really do appreciate that. I understand you had a party last week? Sounds like you are having a good time.

Well, I'd better sign off now. I'll be seeing you soon. Take care.

Love,
Ed

August 6, 1969

Dear Dad and Mom,

It is getting close now. Only a month away as of today. I am now getting all ready to go in every way except that they won't let me hop a plane until the day I'm supposed to leave. I can't figure out why!!

I got a letter from Larry Hicks today. He is down at Fort Benning in Officers Candidate School and seems to be doing fairly well for himself. Larry is the only person I know who gained weight in OCS! Larry talked about his and Diane's baby boy. He seems quite happy. He is also talking about maybe going into some of the extra skills the Army has to offer, like helicopter flight school. Larry's Company Commander at Benning is a guy I knew at Murray State in ROTC.

It is a small Army for officers. You can't go anywhere without running into someone you know. Even now, a man I work with occasionally was Sam Mateer's old Battalion Commander in the 196th Infantry Brigade. He is Colonel Bryant. Ask Sam if he remembers the name.

Sorry I haven't written more often, but I have really been working quite hard the past few weeks and have not had time to do much except sleep and eat. Now that things have eased up, I had a chance to write this letter.

The rains around here have been letting up a little bit this week. It still rains every day, but the sun came out three times so far this week. So, things got dried out a little bit. I'll really be glad to get away from this rain for a long time.

I'd better sign off for now so this letter can get mailed. Take care and remember, I will be coming home VERY soon!

Love,

Ed

Chapter 14

Home Again

I still retained a commitment to the Army for another two years of reserve summer camp and inactive reserve for six years. I went to Summer Camp at Fort Leonard Wood the following year. I was attached to a Minnesota National Guard unit. The guardsmen were for the most part noncombat personnel. They wanted stories, but the six of us who had been overseas were not much in the story telling mood. I was not invited back the following year or any time thereafter.

I decided not to stay in the active reserves. Both George Sheridan and Carey Walker did. Hugh Foster stayed in the active army for the full twenty or more years. Each of them became a at least a Lieutenant Colonel. Joe Rush retired as a Master Sergeant after over 20 years of active duty. Mike Gross became a lineman for the utility company in Missouri until retirement. They were all very good soldiers. Each of the men I served with were good soldiers. Too many of them will stay forever 21 or younger. It was a sad time. Our nation was troubled then and it never accepted those who served during that time. I feel honored that I was a part of serving my country.

Thanks to each of the Soldiers, Sailors, Marines and Air Force people who served.

Welcome Home Brothers!

Thanks!

Acknowledgements

This book has been a long labor It came about when I found the letters I had written to my family and friends in a file my mother Lucille had kept. I was cleaning out their home after their passing and saw the file. Put it aside and months or years later opened and started reading. All my letters to them, my grandmother, family and local friends had been retrieved by Mom and put in this file during the time I was a soldier in Vietnam.

I tried for years to put those letters together with various recollections of my tour. Finally, I decided to preserve them in this book.

I want to thank my family for their support and encouragement. My wife Peggy put up with me staying in the home office typing away.

I bothered Hugh Foster, the current president of the Redcatcher. Org. Hugh was an original member of the 5th Bn 12th Inf and one of the lieutenants during my tour. He was a wealth of information on dates and other officers involved in that year. He was also a retired Army officer (LTC).

George Garin, a friend of Hugh spent time reviewing and proofreading the book and helping me to decide to have it published.

Mike Gross and George Sheridan were both over there with me and have kept in contact. I am proud to know them. There were so many other fine men who I served with during that year. Each of them served, came home and resumed their daily lives. None ever forgot any of their days in Vietnam. God Bless each of them!